CONTROVERSIES IN
PSYCHOANALYTIC METHOD

CONTROVERSIES IN PSYCHOANALYTIC METHOD

From Freud and Ferenczi
to Michael Balint

by
André E. Haynal

translated by
Elizabeth Holder
on the basis of a first draft by
Archie Hooton

with a preface by
Daniel N. Stern

NEW YORK UNIVERSITY PRESS
Washington Square, New York

First published in 1989 in the U.S.A. by
New York University Press
Washington Square
New York, NY 10003
by arrangement with
H. Karnac (Books) Ltd., London, U.K.

Library of Congress Cataloging-in-Publication Data
Haynal, André
   [Technique en question. English]
   Controversies in psychoanalytic method: from Freud and Ferenczi
to Michael Balint/by André E. Haynal: translated by Elizabeth
Holder on the basis of a first draft by Archie Hooton: with a
preface by Daniel N. Stern.
      p.   cm.
   Translation of: La technique en question.
   Includes bibliographical references.
   ISBN 0-8147-3464-2
   1. Psychoanalysis.   I. Title.
RC506.H29513   1989
150.19′5—dc20   89-37535
                                                            CIP

Printed in Great Britain by B.P.C.C. Wheatons Ltd., Exeter

ABOUT THE AUTHOR

Born in 1930, André Haynal studied philosophy and psychology in Budapest, Hungary, followed by medicine in Zurich, Switzerland. He has been trained in neurology, neurosurgery and psychiatry. A practicing psychoanalyst in Geneva, Switzerland, for the past twenty years he spent twice a year as visiting professor at Stanford University in California. He is professor of Psychiatry at the University of Geneva, former President of the Swiss Psychoanalytical Society and former Vice-President of the European Psycho-Analytical Federation. He is the author of several books, including *Depression and Creativity* (New York: International Universities Press); *Abrege de Medecine Psychosomatique* (An Outline of Psychosomatic Medicine) (Paris: Masson); *Fanaticism: A Historical and Psychoanalytical Study* (New York: Schocken Books); and a contributor to *Parental Loss and Achievement* (Eisenstadt et al) (Madison, Connecticut: International Universities Press), all of which have been published in several languages.

ACKNOWLEDGEMENTS

Figure 1, page 40, reproduced with the kind permission of Sigmund Freud's Copyright, Mark Patterson.

Figure 2, page 53, from Dahmer, H.: *Sándor Ferenczi. Zur Erkenntnis des Unbewussten* (Munich: Kindler, 1978), reproduced with the permission of Enid Balint-Edmonds.

Figure 3, page 56, portrait by O. Dormandy (-Székely-Kovacs), reproduced with the permission of Judith Dupont, M.D., Paris.

Figure 4, page 74, photograph by Guy Lavallée, Paris, reproduced by permission.

Figure 5, page 107, kindly lent by Judith Dupont, M.D., Paris.

Figure 6, page 110, kindly lent by Judith Dupont, M.D., Paris.

Figure 7, page 114, reproduced by permission of Judith Dupont, M.D., Paris.

Figure 8, page 116, drawing (1970) by O. Dormandi; published in *Le Coq-Héron*, No. 5 and reproduced with the permission of the publisher.

Figure 9, page 117, drawing, 1970, by O. Dormandi; published in *Le Coq-Héron*, No. 19 and reproduced with the permission of the publisher.

Figures 10 and 11, pages 120/21, caricatures by Stern & Stern and reproduced with the permission of the Balint Archives, Geneva.

Figure 12, page 122, photograph by E. Stein; published in *Patient Centred Medicine*, edited by Philip Hopkins, London: Regional Doctor Publications Ltd., 1972, and reproduced by permission.

Figure 13, page 130, photograph property of Juca Gimes, Zurich; published with the kind permission of Lidia Nemes, Budapest. Also published in: *Le Coq-Héron*, No. 98, 1986, p. 12.

CONTENTS

Illustrations   ix

Foreword   xi

Introduction   xv

1 Prolegomenon: Freud   1

2 The enquiring Sándor Ferenczi   19

3 Intermezzo: Ferenczi—biographical notes   35

4 Psychoanalytic practice in the 1920s and 1930s   61

5 The analyst—the unknown—and his regressed
   patient: the work of Michael Balint   71

   Balint, the analyst / 71
   The search for primary love / 79
   Zones of maturation and of regression / 85
   Transmission in psychoanalysis / 89
   A study of doctors / 92
   In the wake of the controversy surrounding
     Ferenczi / 94
   Balint's scientific position / 97
   Balint, the psychoanalytic investigator / 98

6 From Budapest to London: The life of Michael
Balint   103

7 An emerging perspective of controversies   127

References   145

Appendix A: Congresses of the International
Psychoanalytical Association   161

Appendix B: Bibliography of the works of
Michael Balint, *by Marie-Christine Beck*   163

Appendix C: The spelling of Hungarian names   193

Index   195

ILLUSTRATIONS

Figure 1. Freud and Ferenczi during their holidays in Austria, 1917 / 40

Figure 2. Sándor Ferenczi / 53

Figure 3. Sándor Ferenczi, painting, 1923, by O. Dormandi / 56

Figure 4. Michael Balint working with doctors and psycho-analysts in August 1968 at the Château de Kernuz, Bretagne / 74

Figure 5. Alice Balint / 107

Figure 6. Alice and Michael Balint / 110

Figure 7. Enid and Michael Balint at the beginning of the 1960s / 114

Figure 8. Michael Balint, drawing, 1970, by O. Dormandi / 116

Figure 9. Enid Balint, drawing, 1970, by O. Dormandi / 117

Figure 10. Caricature by Stern & Stern, from a felicitation document addressed to M. Balint for his 70th birthday, 3 December 1966 / 120

Figure 11. Caricature by Stern & Stern, from a felicitation document addressed to M. Balint for his 70th birthday, 3 December 1966 / 121

Figure 12. Michael Balint / 122

Figure 13. The Hungarian Psychoanalytical Group, July 1928, on the occasion of the 55th birthday of Ferenczi / 130

FOREWORD

André Haynal gives us a perspective on the history of psychoanalysis, and much more, in this multifaceted and remarkable book. Several stories and lines of inquiry are woven together. There is the story of the Budapest School of psychoanalysis and its impact. Within and around that story, there are accounts of the lives and works of Ferenczi and Balint, who provided the core of the Budapest School. There is the omnipresent history of some of the great—and continuing—controversies in psychoanalysis. These controversies are seen in the light of the conflicting natures and approaches between the Budapest School and its descendants, on the one hand, and Freud and his direct descendants on the other hand. And finally, there is Haynal's view of the nature of the psychoanalytic movement and endeavor that emerges from his weaving these fascinating stories together.

Haynal is uniquely placed to do all this. He is Hungarian-born, and his sense of person and place is never impersonal. Like the best of the Budapest School, he is not a passive mirror to reflect its history. He has also been privileged to have access to important and revealing unpublished material both from the Freud–Ferenczi correspondence and from the Balint Archives. There is new history here. At the same time, while he has worked largely in Europe, he has also worked and visited extensively in the United States and is thoroughly familiar with current intellectual trends on both sides of the Atlantic. This is crucial because his accounts constantly address present issues that define or contrast different current psychoanalytic 'schools' or factions. And, thankfully, he is an artful story teller, so that the strands of history that he takes in hand come together and come alive to illuminate the present.

As an American, with my own particular interests, there are several aspects of this book that struck me in particular. I will dwell on these. (The book is rich enough for each reader to do the same.)

Working in North America, it is impossible not to be aware of the influence of Budapest in psychoanalysis—both through reading the basic major thinkers and through inevitable contact with the many emigrants that Hungary provided to enrich psychoanalysis in America. Having trained at the Columbia Psychoanalytic Center, where the presence of Sandor Rado is still alive, I was well aware of the direct heritage. A shortened list of names tells much: Sandor Rado, Franz Alexander, Theresa Benedek, Thomas Szasz, John Gedo, Sandor Feldman, Robert Bak, David Rappaport, Sandor Lorand, Géza Róheim (and this makes no mention of the indirect descendants).

Haynal has defined and traced some of the common strains that characterized the Budapest School, so that one emerges from this book with an integrated view of its influence and a greater appreciation of its far-reaching impact. And this brings us to the great controversy that began between Freud and Ferenczi and was continued in the work of Balint.

Haynal describes this controversy in terms of the initial form it took, a disagreement about experimenting with technique and Ferenczi placing the analytic situation more squarely at the center of inquiry. Haynal also places this conflict in its personal context of the relationship between Freud and Ferenczi. But most valuable of all, he then elaborates upon the full implications of the controversy, and we discover this split to be at the heart of the major questions still at issue in psychoanalysis: emphasis on technique versus on metapsychology; direct experience versus insight; process versus content; the patient's subjectivity versus the 'scientific' theory; empathy versus interpretation; a psychology of one person (the patient) versus a psychology of two people, the patient–therapist dyad, transference and counter-transference and the 'real' relationship. In revealing the ramifications of the controversy in its ever-spreading consequences, we find ourselves viewing the living history behind the major issues re-raised by Kohut, by Lacan, by the various object-relations theories, by the position of psychoanalysis as the co-construction of narrative, and others.

In this light, the seminal importance of the Budapest School takes on larger dimensions, and we are forced to reevaluate, in part, our intellectual ancestry.

My own particular interests have long been in infant and child development and its conceptualization in psychoanalysis. In that area alone one immediately encounters the direct and indirect influence of the Budapest School in Melanie Klein, Balint, Spitz, Mahler, and Winnicott. And what Haynal made clear for me was how Ferenczi's and then Balint's insistence on a 'two-person psychology' for psychoanalysis was the precursor to an approach that placed the mutual interaction between infant and mother at the very center in understanding psychic development. And this was indispensable.

Finally, in unravelling these strands and weaving them together as he does, Haynal ends up by presenting a clearer way to view constructively the current pluralism that now exists in psychoanalysis. In providing this clearer view, Haynal, himself, takes a place in the grand tradition of the

Budapest School, as a creative explorer of the psychoanalytic situation, of the psychoanalytic method—but from the historical viewpoint.

Daniel N. Stern, M.D.

Instructor, Columbia Psychoanalytic Center
Professor of Psychiatry, Brown University
Professor Extraordinaire of Psychology, University of Geneva

INTRODUCTION

Throughout his history man has struggled to suppress his sorrows, discomfort and inner conflicts. In order to overcome this lack of well-being and to explore his inner world, he turned in the past to religions and philosophies. Twentieth-century man turns rather to psychoanalysis, a by-product of the great secular discoveries of the nineteenth century, in the tradition of the biological and physiological advances made by such men as Darwin, Brücke and Fechner, to the German and English philosophies established by the searching minds of Goethe, Kant, Nietzsche and John Stuart Mill, to the sociology of Auguste Comte and to the Clinic of Charcot and Bernheim.

The precursors of psychoanalysis and the impact of Freud on the history of European thought have been extensively examined by several authors: Ellenberger (1970), Kaufman (1980), Assoun (1981), Chertok and de Saussure (1973). There is no need therefore to dwell further on these aspects of psychoanalytic history.

The main goal of this book is to explore the development of psychoanalysis as a *method*, and the controversies such a development aroused *within* the group formed by its first practitioners. Theirs were ambitious aims: to capture, to define, to locate and to name the forces at work in the innermost recesses of the human mind; then to create a scientific framework and so gradually reach an understanding of the nature of these forces.

Achieving such aims was no easy matter. Freud sought to establish the criteria for his new discipline either by correlating it with the biological sciences—he seems to have believed throughout his life that biologists would one day substantiate concepts such as quanta of energy—or with the changes in behaviour brought about by his interventions, which would validate his theory. But what if there were *another order of truth*? 'The history of science is science itself.' Perhaps this is nowhere more true than in the field of psychoanalysis. A longitudinal, historical survey of the evolution of certain problems and the controversies they have engendered may further our understanding of the nature of psychoanalytic practice and help to define the scientific theory founded upon it. It is the first part of a study aimed at exploring the difficulties inherent in psychoanalytic 'techniques'.

Although the present volume is intended as a history of *ideas*, we have included a chapter devoted to the biography of Ferenczi, and another to that of Balint. The purpose of these biographies is to provide little-known facts from the lives and background of these two men, which shed light on developments in psychoanalysis. This study begins with Freud's own practice of psychoanalysis and what he had to say about it, and goes on to retrace the controversy between Sigmund Freud and Sándor Ferenczi, as well as the work of Michael Balint, Ferenczi's main disciple and successor. Balint transplanted from Budapest to London a school of thought important for psychoanalytic practice, which profoundly influenced those analysts known collectively as 'The British Middle Group', or as 'The Independents' to distinguish them from 'Freudians' and 'Kleinians'. Balint is also the first to have comprehended what is actually at stake in theoretical controversies.

Although the history of analytic affiliations may shed considerable light on contemporary analytic practice in Europe, the wide dispersal of European analysts in the wake of world events makes exhaustive reconstruction difficult. This study is limited, therefore, to following one thread in the tapestry of psychoanalysis—that of the Budapest School. It does not pretend to portray the history of psychoanalytic technique in its entirety. It covers neither the period after 1950, nor alternative theories and techniques outside the main current of Freudian thought, such as those represented by the work of Harry Stack Sullivan or the Washington School. Its aim is to follow the development of approaches to the unconscious discernible in the analytic situation. I hope that this book might present a history of ideas contributing to a renewed understanding of modern man's great adventure, psychoanalysis.

For my study and the writing of this book, I was fortunate enough to be able to refer to the personal notes and correspondence of the late Dr. Michael Balint, currently housed in the *Balint Archives* in Geneva. I had access to unpublished sources such as the correspondence between Sigmund Freud and Sándor Ferenczi, through the good offices of the Committee for the Publication of the Freud–Ferenczi Correspondence, whose members include Enid Balint of London, Judith Dupont of Paris, Ilse Grubrich-Simitis of Frankfurt am Main, Mark Paterson of London, Arthur Rosenthal of Boston and the author. This correspondence is housed in the Austrian National Library in Vienna. The writings of Freud, Ferenczi, Balint and others, as well as the reminiscences of those who experienced those times, have been of the utmost importance for my work.

I wish to extend my thanks in the first place to Mrs. Enid Balint of London, for having generously donated her late husband's handwritten notes, letters and other material.

This gift made it possible to set up the *Balint Archives* mentioned above.

I acknowledge my indebtedness to Professor John Balint of Albany, New York; Mr. Louis Barton of Brighton, Great Britain; Dr. Andrew Petö of New York City and Dr. Livia Nemes of Budapest, all of whom supplied numerous details on Michael Balint and the Hungarian psychoanalytic group. Dr. Judith Dupont of Paris placed important documents at my disposal and was ever readily available to respond to my many questions and requests.

Marie-Christine Beck, clinical psychologist, classified the documents included in the *Balint Archives*. Her notes on this documentation as well as her bibliography of the works of Michael Balint (Appendix B) have proved of inestimable service in my work. Together with Dora Heer and Maud Struchen, she undertook innumerable bibliographical searches.

My thanks also go to Mr. André Baudet, head librarian of the Medical Library of the Psychiatric Institutions of the University of Geneva; Ms. Brigitte Weyermann, librarian at the Center for Psychoanalysis in Zurich, and the many others who helped to establish a complete list of the works of Michael Balint.

This study was carried out in close collaboration with Maud Struchen who, for the past fifteen years, has helped me assiduously in my scientific work; without her help, I would never have reached the publication stage.

My thanks go to Dr. Archie Hooton for the first draft of this translation. For the final version, my very special gratitude goes to Mrs. Elizabeth Holder (London). I would like to express my gratefulness for the very careful publishing to Mr. Cesare D. S. Sacerdoti, Karnac Books, London, and to Ms. Klara Majthényi King, Communication Crafts, East Grinstead, Sussex, England.

The University of Geneva (Switzerland) and its Psychiatric Institutions enabled me to dedicate part of my time to this study. Writing was facilitated by my stays at Stanford

University in California, by the Chairman of the Department of Psychiatry and Behavioral Sciences, Thomas A. Gonda M.D., and my friends and colleagues there: Professor A. F. Koerner (Stanford), Professor R. Blum (Stanford), and Dr. E. Blum (Stanford), Professor W. Lederer (Berkeley) and Dr. A. Lederer-Botwin (San Francisco), among many others.

My wife, Veronique Haynal-Reymond, provided me, as always, with the loving environment and unfailing support without which I would not have been able to work.

My heartfelt thanks to one and all.

A.H.

CONTROVERSIES IN
PSYCHOANALYTIC METHOD

CHAPTER ONE

Prolegomenon: Freud

There is no inductive method which leads to the fundamental concepts of physics.

Albert Einstein

One can only study what has first been dreamed. Science is formed more on reverie than on experiments and we need experiments to clear away the mists of our dreams.

Gaston Bachelard

Freud defined psychoanalysis as 'a conversation between two people' (Freud, 1904a, *7*:249). 'Nothing takes place between them except that they talk to each other' (Freud, 1926e, *20*:187). Though apt, such definitions obviously have their limitations. To the 'conversation between two people' must be added the frame of reference of the one who listens, his familiarity with the workings of the unconscious mind and his knowledge of transference and resistance (Freud, 1914d, *14*:16; 1923a, *18*:246), which are the cornerstones of psychoanalysis. Freud wrote to Groddeck, 'Whoever recognizes that transference and resistance are the pivot of treatment belongs irrevocably to our savage horde' (Freud, 1960a, letter dated 5 June 1917).

Freud formulated a few guidelines designed to facilitate the encounter that he called psychoanalysis. 'This technique is the only one suited to my individuality', he said. 'I do not venture to deny that another physician, differently constituted, might find himself driven to adopt a different attitude' (Freud, 1912e, *12*:111). Later he was to add: 'I

1

think I am well-advised to call these rules "recommenda-tions" and not to claim any unconditional acceptance for them' (Freud, 1913c, *12*:123).[1] For decades following publication of these statements, the unanswered—and perhaps unanswerable—question about technique fired controversies over psychoanalytic theory and practice and the links between them. Throughout his career, however, Freud himself continued to take a dim view of those who 'take precepts literally or exaggerate them' (Freud, 1963a, letter to Pfister dated 22 October 1927). Indeed, early in his analytic career he had recognized that technique as it was then practised would have to be 'modified in certain ways' (Freud, 1910d, *11*:145) as knowledge accumulated, and he foresaw that the technical problems were in connection with the therapist himself and with his difficulties, i.e. under-standing his own feelings.

In dealing with the subject of psychoanalytic technique, Freud was sometimes ambiguous. In private he was not beyond devaluing the carefully worded formulations he laid down in his technical writings or decrying rules as mere guidelines for beginners. He reportedly told Smiley Blan-ton: 'Of course, beginners probably need something to go on. ... But, ... then they must learn to develop their own technique' (Blanton, 1971, p. 48). As yet, there is no evidence that serious thought has been given to identifying those factors that make technique personal.

The other real or apparent ambiguity is to be found in the contradiction between Freud's *practice* as we know it from his case records and his analysands' recall on the one hand, and his 'official' *position* as it appears in his technical writings, on the other.

When Freud was still using hypnosis to explore the mind and, subsequently, catharsis as treatment, the question that emerged was, what motivates the desire for change and how does one account for the emotional *impact* of the processes brought into play by the two protagonists. The use of new concepts such as transference and counter-trans-ference, however, raised a further question: how to identify the forces that perpetuate the repetition compulsion in analysis and how to modify them.

Perhaps under the sway of the German romanticism to which he was heir, Freud yearned to understand the human mind, to discover what lies beneath its surface, what lurks in its 'depths'. He concentrated all his scientific efforts on uncovering the law governing the invisible, the intangible. 'I am interested only in the unconscious', he is reported to have told Melanie Klein (M. Spira, personal communication). He called this hidden dimension of the mind the 'id', as Nietzsche and Groddeck had before him. Although in this he did no more than succumb to the German philosophical tradition embodied in the thinking of such men as Feuerbach, Kant, Lichtenberg (cf. Will, 1985), Freud followed in the footsteps of his teachers Brücke, Helmholtz and others by creating a scientific rather than a philosophical foundation for his ideas, thus departing radically from the German romantic tradition, which had tended to steer medicine in the direction of vitalism. In the final analysis, it is a far cry from romanticism and vitalism to exploring dreams in order to discover their natural laws or approaching the unconscious in order to make it conscious, or working so that 'where Id was, there Ego shall be' (Freud, 1933a, 22:80). It was undoubtedly this trend that enabled Freud to reach previously unknown territory and add to mankind's accumulated fund of objective knowledge. Having begun his career by thinking of himself as a 'conquistador' (letter to Fliess dated 1 February 1900, in Masson, 1985, p. 398), he was in a position towards the end of his life to point out proudly that psychoanalysis had revealed 'rules and laws which bring order into chaos' (Freud, 1937c, 23:228).

Although Freud was passionately interested in theoretical exploration, he did not always show the same enthusiasm for clinical technique and the unique relation between analyst and patient. His own testimony bears this out. In his 'New Introductory Lectures' he wrote, 'I have never been a therapeutic enthusiast' (Freud, 1933a, 22:151). He once said to Kardiner, 'I have no great interest in therapeutic problems. I am much too impatient now. I have several handicaps that disqualify me as a great analyst' (Kardiner, 1977, p. 69). Indirect evidence in support of this view is contained in a letter Ferenczi wrote to Freud: 'I do not share your opinion that treatment is negligible or unimportant, and that it could be dispensed with because it bears less interest for us. I have also often felt "fed up" with clinical practice, but I have always overcome the feeling, and I can happily assure you that it is precisely at that moment [when the feeling is overcome] that a whole series of problems appear in a different light, more clearly perhaps even the problem of repression' (J. Dupont, 1985, p. 25). 'Technical progress will advance theory', might have been Ferenczi's motto. 'Developing theory will further technique', would have been Freud's reply. But despite these indications to the contrary, Freud was in fact keenly aware of how important clinical observation was for the substantiation of his theories. 'As you know, psychoanalysis originated as a method of treatment; it has far outgrown this, but it has not abandoned its home-ground and it is still linked to its contact with patients for increasing its depth and for its further development. The accumulated *impressions* from which we *derive our theories* could be arrived at in no other way' (Freud, 1933a, *22*:151 [italics added]).

We may consider that Freud completed the basic framework of the psychoanalytic method between 1895 and 1900 (e.g., Gill, 1982, Vol. 1, p. 2; Lipton, 1977), but when he was still exploring his chosen field of investigation in 1895, he thought of himself as a scientific pioneer and considered his patients as his 'collaborators' (Freud, 1895a[2]).

By explaining things [to the patient], by giving him information about the marvellous world of psychical processes into which we ourselves only gained insight by such analyses, we make him himself into a collaborator, induce him to regard himself with the objective interest of an investigator, and thus push back his resistance, resting as it does on an affective basis. .... One works to the best of one's power, as an elucidator (where ignorance has given rise to fear), as a teacher, as the representative of a freer or superior view of the world, as a father confessor who gives absolution as it were, by a continuance of his sympathy and respect after the confession has been made (Freud, 1895d, 2:282).

It was not until the concept of *transference* had been worked out that this basic theoretical framework changed. Freud used the new concept in an attempt to correlate what he had learned from his experience of hypnosis with the phenomena arising out of this new way of listening and understanding (cf. Freud, 1916–1917, *16*:451). In the Dora case (1905) he asked,

What are transferences? They are new editions or facsimiles of the impulses and phantasies which are aroused and made conscious during the progress of the analysis; but they have this peculiarity, which is characteristic for their species, that they replace some earlier person by the person of the physician. To put it another way: a whole series of psychological experiences are revived, not as belonging to the past, but as applying to the person of the physician at the present moment.

A few lines later, Freud points out how transference must be combatted.

It becomes evident that transference is an inevitable necessity. Practical experience, at all events, shows conclusively that *there is no means of avoiding it,* and that this latest creation of the disease must be *combatted* like all the earlier ones' (Freud, 1905e, 7:116 [italics added]).

Going more deeply into his discovery, he observes that 'The psycho-analytic treatment does not *create* transferences, it merely brings them to light, like so many other hidden psychical factors' (ibid., 7:117). He returned to the subject in 'An autobiographical study': 'Transference is merely uncovered and isolated by analysis. It is a universal phenomenon of the human mind, it decides the success of all medical influence, and in fact dominates the whole of each person's relations to his human environment' (Freud, 1925d, 20:42).

Even after Freud had discovered the fundamental role transference plays in treatment, it was accepted and applied only gradually and not without difficulty. 'The transference is indeed a cross', he said (Freud, 1963a, letter to Pfister dated 5 June 1910). Similarly, in 'The Rat Man' he speaks of 'the painful road of transference' (Freud, 1909d, 10:209). In a letter dated 15 February 1924 (Freud, 1965a), he confessed to Abraham that he *feared* repetition in analysands and that he appreciated the 'amendment' proposed by Ferenczi and Rank stressing the usefulness of the experience in analysis. He repeatedly insisted that transference phenomena pose the greatest difficulty for the analyst, but that they 'do us the inestimable service of making the patient's hidden and forgotten erotic impulses immediate and manifest. For when all is said and done, it is impossible to destroy anyone *in absentia* or *in effigie*' (Freud, 1912b, 12:108). Although the key importance of transference had been acknowledged, its limits, if there were any in the analytic process, and the necessity of *interpreting* it and to what extent, were not yet clear. How earlier discoveries about the unconscious would be manifested in the transference would only gradually be understood (Freud, 1912b, 12:105). It took time for psychoanalysis to cover the distance between 'The interpretation of dreams' (Freud, 1900a, 4/5:1–261) and 'The *handling* of dream interpretation *in psychoanalysis*' (Freud, 1911e, 12:89–96 [italics added]).

Freud never departed from his role of scientific observer, as 'scout of the unconscious'. His theoretical writings, his published case records and the reminiscences of his former analysands make this abundantly clear. For instance, he told Hilda Doolittle that he did not like the maternal transference, adding 'I feel so masculine' (Doolittle, 1956, p. 147), and he avoided contact with psychotics on the grounds that 'cooperation of this kind habitually fails with psychotic patients' (Freud, 1937c, 23:235). Lipton (1977) is undoubtedly right in claiming that for Freud transference never became an exclusive instrument for understanding and maintaining the therapeutic process. He reminds us that Freud's activity was never restricted to interpretation but that he also formed a 'personal non technical relationship' with his patients. Freud himself said that 'Not every good relation between analyst and analysand, during and after analysis, should automatically be evaluated as transference. It would seem that certain of these friendly relations rest on genuine foundations and are viable' (Freud, 1937c, 23:222). Lipton recalls that Freud gave Dr. Paul Lorenz, the famous 'Rat Man', a meal on 28 December 1907 (Lipton, 1977, pp. 259, 264; Freud, 1974, p. 210), and that later on he sent him a postcard (Freud, 1974, p. 180) and lent him a book (ibid., p. 218). Lipton also points out that in 1924 Freud added a footnote to the published case of Emmy von N. to the effect that no analyst could read it without smiling (Freud, 1895d, 2:105, footnote). He did not, however, make such an addition to the subsequent reprints of the 'Rat Man' case (Freud, 1909d, 10:151–249, with additions from 1923, 10:212, 235, 249, and from 1924, 10: 214, 221). Lipton's point (1977) is that there is no indication that Freud modified his technique during the course of his life as a result of his work on transference.

It is worth recalling, in this connection, the testimonies of his analysands, despite the inevitable subjectivity of their reminiscences in an area as emotionally loaded as their own analyses.

For Money-Kyrle, Freud's technique

was exactly what it is now though a little less strict; he did occasionally depart from transference interpretations. But this was so rare that I can only think of two

examples: his illustrating a point about the primal scene
with a bit of material from another patient ending with
'You would like her. She is a princess', implying, I
suppose, that he thought me a snob, and of course I very
soon knew who she was. ... The other example was his
taking me into the next room to show me his Euchaptis[3]
to explain that their colour was fading because they had
been dug up like relics from the unconscious' (Money-
Kyrle, 1979, p. 267).

For Jeanne Lampl-de Groot, Freud's early recommendations that the analyst serve as a mirror on to which the
patient can project his hidden conflicts (Freud, 1912e,
12:118) 'were primarily meant to forestall burdening the
patient with the analyst's personal affects, problems and
conflicts' (Lampl-de Groot, 1976, p. 284). She feels she was
greatly influenced as an analyst by Freud's 'carefully
selected alternation of "strict neutrality" and human
relatedness' (ibid.).

At times, Freud was very direct, communicating his own
feelings to his patients. Hilda Doolittle describes Freud's
temper as he pounded 'with his hand, with his fist, on the
head-piece of the old-fashioned horsehair sofa' (Doolittle,
1956, passim). Freud said to her on another occasion, 'I am
an old man—you do not think it worth while to love me'
(ibid., p. 62). HD's memoirs of her analysis suggest that in
his work, Freud was very direct, sometimes bordering on
being brutally frank, and gave the impression of a
master–pupil relationship. Ruitenbeek remarks that Freud
'ignored what has become the orthodox pattern of non-
interference. On the contrary, he was chatty, sometimes
even gossipy'[4] (Ruitenbeek, 1973, p. 19).

Alix Strachey, known for her scholarly contributions to
*The Standard Edition of the Complete Psychological Works
of Sigmund Freud,* which she carried on after her husband's
death, also had vivid recollections of her analysis with
Freud. Masud Khan recalls an anecdote she once told him:

It had been a critical week in her analysis, which resulted in her having a significant dream. She recounted her dream to the Professor and they worked around it. Then the Professor gave an interpretation, at the end of which he got up to fetch a cigar for himself, saying, 'Such insights need celebrating'. Alix Strachey mildly protested that she had not yet told the whole dream, to which the Professor replied, 'Don't be greedy, that is enough insight for one week!' (Khan, 1973, p. 370).

Altogether his remarks suggest an atmosphere where occasionally the direct expression of the analyst's feelings can be made without undue concern about a 'neutral' analyst. Freud's interventions suggest that his relationship with his patients was a pupil–teacher one. 'Psycho-analytic treatment is a kind of after-education', he affirmed (Freud, 1916–1917, *16*:451). Referring to a patient he felt had unconsciously expressed hostile feelings toward him by leaving his office door ajar (as if to say he felt that nobody other than he would come to this analyst), Freud recommends giving patients 'a sharp reprimand' to keep them from behaving impolitely and disrespectfully (ibid., *16*:247). It may have been that in making this statement Freud was merely giving expression to the mores prevalent in Vienna in his time. Or it could have been that his practice was ultimately confined almost exclusively to training analysts. 'I hardly take patients now but only pupils', he wrote to Abraham in 1924 (Freud, 1965a, letter dated 15 February 1924). It could also have been that many of his pupils were unable to remain in Vienna for a lengthy period of time, and so his practice with them was a sort of brief training analysis in the belief that in such conditions, treatment could only be 'short and incomplete', but that it would give the student 'a firm conviction of the existence of the unconscious' and 'a first sample of the technique which has proved to be the only effective one in analytic work' (Freud, 1937c, *23*:248).[5]

Perhaps some of Freud's comments were related to the fact that he was talking to analysands who were 'pupils' at the same time. He told one, 'In reading articles about analysis, look at the date of the article' (Blanton, 1971, p. 51). Perhaps he was sometimes so 'active ... in analysing ... dreams' (ibid., p. 53) because that was his current project. According to Raymond de Saussure, Freud

> had practiced suggestion too long not to have been materially affected by it. When he was persuaded of the truth of something, he had considerable difficulty in waiting until this became clear to his patient. Freud wanted to convince him immediately. Because of that, he talked too much. ... [It was easy to sense the] special theoretical question [uppermost in his mind] for often during the analytic hour he developed at length new points of view he was clarifying in his mind. This was a gain for the intellect but not always for the patient's treatment' (de Saussure, 1956, pp. 357–359 [re-translated]).

Blanton reports that Freud made comments such as, 'You were much freer (today) than before' (Blanton, 1971, p. 27), or remarks like, 'That is very interesting. You must be patient. We will get to the deeper layers, and then I shall not be so silent, I shall give more of myself' (ibid., p. 28). There is the constantly recurring image of Freud as a reassuring schoolmaster teaching and explaining, 'You see how much more interesting it is when you associate to your dreams' (ibid., p. 31); and 'For an analyst, not to tell his dreams is a nice bit of resistance' (ibid., p. 30).

These attitudes may seem contrary to the rule that transference should be consistently interpreted. Nor does the detached attitude of the surgeon recommended by Freud (Freud, 1912e, *12*:115) appear in these reports either. Some authors have subsequently seen fit to level criticism at Freud's own technique. His handling of the 'Rat Man' is one case in point. Kris thought that it was a 'conspicuous intellectual indoctrination' (Kris, 1951, p. 17). Kanzer agrees with Kris that Freud did not clearly perceive the therapeutic implications of the patient's feelings toward the analyst (Kanzer, 1952, passim). Zetzel is of the opinion that Freud was unable or unwilling to limit his interventions 'to the interpretation of the transference neurosis' (Zetzel, 1966, p. 128). It has also been pointed out that Freud overlooked the impact the analyst's extra-transferential interventions might have on patients. Freud assured the 'Wolf Man', for instance, that a troublesome symptom he complained of would be cured by analysis. 'This intervention was never resolved through interpretation' (Gedo and Goldberg, 1973, p. 187) and although the patient was temporarily relieved of the symptom, he subsequently returned to Freud on more than one occasion with the same complaint.

Kardiner's comment is in the same vein: 'The man who had invented the concept of transference did not recognize it when it occurred. ... He overlooked one thing: *Yes, I was afraid of my father in childhood, but the one whom I feared now was Freud himself.* He could make me or break me, which my father no longer could. ... He pushed the entire relation into the past, thereby making the analysis a historical reconstruction' (Kardiner, 1977, p. 58).[6] So, once again, the question of the limits of transference is raised. There is an interesting anecdote in this connection. Freud had given Blanton, then in analysis with him, a four-volume set of his *Collected Papers*. In the following session he took up this fact by remarking that 'There is a change in the transference. It is probably due to the present of the books. You will see from this what difficulties gifts in analysis always make' (Blanton, 1971, p. 42).

Although Freud wrote convincingly of the importance of counter-transference and the need to analyse it, he expressed reservations about it on other occasions. 'He believed that personal analysis was necessary as preparation for analytic work, but indicated that rare, very balanced individuals, like Abraham, could do without. He strongly urged not fractional analysis, but a return for a new analysis after five-year intervals' (Grinker, 1940, p. 183). Boss notes with astonishment, 'During the entire time I was privileged to be in analysis with him, he acted quite differently to what one would have expected ... from his views on the analyst as a mirror'. Boss goes on, 'He hastened to reduce his fees to a minimum as soon as he learned that I was going hungry in order to pay him. More than once he gave me ten schillings out of his own pocket' (Boss, 1973, pp. 81–82). Boss adds—and this is an interesting remark—that his analyst in Zurich at the time, Hans B. Eichenburg, applied Freud's technical recommendations much more strictly than Freud himself.

Kardiner says that Freud sometimes mentioned personal matters to people in analysis with him: family preoccupations, the death of his daughter Sophie, Anna's analysis, her hesitancy to get engaged. He also reports that Strachey and Rickman were intrigued to hear that Freud sometimes made small talk with his analysands. '[To us] he never says a word', Rickman said (Kardiner, 1977, p. 78). In his book, Kardiner relates another episode that leads us to believe that Freud acted out his counter-transference.

Oberndorf got to be on bad terms with Freud on the very first day of his analysis, because he came prepared with a dream, which he related in the very first hour. The dream was as follows: He was riding in a carriage pulled by two horses, one of which was white, and the other black. They were going to some unknown destination. Traveling to an unknown destination as an opening dream in analysis is not infrequent. But this particular dream happened, rightly or wrongly, to hit upon one of Oberndorf's apparent weak spots, because it was Freud's interpretation that he, Oberndorf, could never marry because he didn't know whether to choose a white woman or a black woman, and so he was in a quandary. He was not married then, nor did he ever marry, and he was a Southerner. He was born in Atlanta, Georgia, and had been raised by a

black 'mammy'. This interpretation infuriated Oberndorf, and they haggled about this dream for months, until
Freud got tired of it and discontinued the analysis. Freud
was unequivocal in his condemnation of Oberndorf's
character and of his ability, and later on he even refused
to write a preface for a book he had written (ibid., pp.
75–76).

This does seem like an acting out of the counter-
transference by Freud, and it is interesting to mention that,
according to Natterson (1966), he would have advocated,
on some occasions, the use of role-play by the analyst as
Alexander recommended later: 'Freud's capacities as
psychoanalytic consultant were evident when, for instance,
Reik had difficulty in eliciting transference feelings from a
female patient. Freud's advice was simple, "Make her
jealous". So, on the next occasion, as this patient was
leaving, Reik warmly greeted the next patient—also a
woman—in the hearing of the problem patient. During the
following session, the previously aloof patient became
furious with Reik and freely expressed her anger, and the
analysis proceeded more effectively' (ibid., p. 256). In the
same article, we read that 'Reik also learned the technique
of interrupting analysis for therapeutic purposes from
Freud, who talked about "fractured [sic] analysis", in which
interruptions necessitated by the patient's travels were
discovered to have therapeutic value' (ibid.).

The foregoing examples show that Freud was rather
uncertain about the theoretical and practical *consequences*
of his fundamental discovery of transference. In some way,
this uncertainty must have accounted, at least in part, for
Freud's distaste for the maternal transference and for his
aversion to psychotic patients.

But Freud was not the only one to complain about the
discomforts of being personally exposed to transference.
Sándor Ferenczi, the man who debated this issue with
Freud more often than anyone else, speaks of 'the withering
heat of transference', which, however, he considered neces-

sary if the analyst is to acquire 'essentially new knowledge about himself' (Ferenczi and Groddeck, 1982, p. 71). During his analysis of Dora, Freud came to see transference as 'an artificial illness which is at every point accessible to our interventions' (Freud, 1914g, 12:154). As he developed his understanding of the analyst–analysand relationship toward the end of the first decade of the century, he began to conceive the notion of split-off parts, separated from the ego, by which he at first alluded both to repression and to splitting in its subsequent connotation. 'The great unity we call ... ego', he writes, 'fits into itself all the instinctual impulses which before had been split off and held apart from it' (Freud, 1919a, 17:161). The second topographical model enabled him to formulate one of the motives of treatment as a superego rendered gentler by the more tolerant superego of the analyst (Freud, 1940a, 23:172ff.). In so doing, he translates the theme of 'confessor' and of 'absolution' into metapsychological terms (ibid., 23:174). He pursues this line of thought: 'The analytic physician and the patient's weakened ego, basing themselves on the real external world, have to bond themselves together into a party against the enemies: the instinctual demands of the id and the conscientious demands of the superego. We form a pact with each other. ... This pact constitutes the analytic situation' (ibid., 23:173). He also states, 'the analytic situation consists in our allying ourselves with the ego of the person undergoing treatment, in order to subdue portions of his id which are uncontrolled—that is to say to include them in the synthesis of his ego' (Freud, 1937c, 23:235).

There are other, less explicit models in Freud's writings. In 'The Dynamics of Transference' (Freud, 1912b, 12:97–108) he expresses the idea that the analytic process is characterized by the patient's struggle to hold on to archaic objects; transference helps the patient simultaneously to hold on and to abandon them. Here we find the germ of a later theory about internal objects and of a study of their abandonment, viz. mourning, a theme taken up in 'Mourning and Melancholia' (Freud, 1917e, *14*:237–258; Haynal, 1976, Chapter 5, passim).

Deeper exploration of the dimensions of transference in the patient–analyst relationship opens new perspectives. 'We allow him access to the transference, that playground where he can be himself with almost total freedom, and where we ask him to reveal any and everything pathogenic that lurks in his mind' (Freud, 1914g, *12*:154).[7] 'Providing only that the patient shows compliance enough to respect the necessary conditions of the analysis, we shall regularly succeed in giving all the symptoms of the illness a new transference meaning and in replacing his ordinary neurosis by a "transference neurosis" of which he can be cured by the therapeutic work. The transference thus creates a kind of *intermediary region* between illness and real life through which the transition from the one to the other is made. ... At the same time, it is a *piece of real experience* made possible by especially favorable conditions, and it is of a *provisional* nature' [italics added]. This 'piece of real experience' brings memories alive and confronts the patient with his resistances. 'From the repetition reactions which are exhibited in the transference we are led along the familiar paths to the awakening of the memories, which appear, without difficulty as it were, after the resistances have been overcome' (Freud, 1914g, *12*:154–155). By 1914, then, Freud had reached an understanding of transference as experience, a point of view that, as we shall see, he attributed to Ferenczi. This formulation already shows the similarities between their thinking, as well as how frequently Freud's opinion on these issues vacillated.

By 1910 Freud had devised a concept of countertransference, the complement to transference as he had formulated it in 1905. 'We have become aware of the "counter-transference" that arises in him [the physician] as a result of the patient's influence on his unconscious feelings, and are almost inclined to insist that he shall recognize this counter-transference in himself and overcome it.' He immediately linked this with the analyst's own analysis. 'We consequently require that he shall begin his activity with a self-analysis and continually carry it deeper while he is making his observations on his patients' (Freud, 1910d, *11*:144–145).

Two years later, with that extreme mobility of thought that was his strength, Freud had come to understand that counter-transference, like transference, is a valuable *instrument* for—rather than a hindrance to—the analyst. He wrote:

> To put it in a formula: he [the analyst] must turn his own unconscious like a receptive organ towards the transmitting unconscious of the patient. He must adjust himself to the patient as a telephone receiver is adjusted to the transmitting microphone. Just as the receiver converts back into sound waves the electric oscillations in the telephone line which were set up by sound waves, so the doctor's unconscious is able, from the derivatives of the unconscious which are communicated to him, to reconstruct that unconscious, which has determined the patient's free associations. But if the doctor is to be in a position to use his unconscious in this way as an instrument in the analysis, he must himself fulfil one psychological condition to a high degree. He may not tolerate any resistances in himself. ... (Freud, 1912e, *12*:115–116).

This aspect of Freud's work and practice, as we have just attempted to reconstitute it, remains riddled with unresolved questions heatedly debated in analytic circles. Although differences in psychological make-up may account to a large extent for the differences of opinion on these unsettled aspects of psychoanalysis, the very fact that debates still rage underlines the *relevance* of these issues to psychoanalytic practice. The first such divergence was the Freud–Ferenczi controversy.

Ferenczi greatly expanded the concept of transference. 'I ... regard *every* dream, *every* gesture, *every* parapraxis, *every* aggravation or improvement in the condition of the patient as above all an expression of transference and resistance.' He quotes Groddeck 'who, when the condition of one of his patients is aggravated always comes forward with the stereotyped question: "What have you against me, what have I done to you?" He asserted that by the solving of this question the aggravation of symptoms could always be removed, and that also with the help of such analytic devices he was able to understand more deeply the previous history of the case' (Ferenczi, 1926 [271], *FUR.*, pp. 225–226).*

This conception of transference led Ferenczi to discover in his own way the importance of experience.

Our own writings sketch in this sense the beginning of a phase we are inclined to contrast with the preceding by calling it the *phase of experience*. Whereas, formerly, attempts were made to achieve a therapeutic effect via the patient's reactions to [the analyst's] explanations, we now prefer to harness all knowledge obtained through psychoanalysis entirely to the treatment process by directly *provoking*, based on our insight, adequate *experiences* and by limiting ourselves to explaining to the patient only the ones which are, naturally, also immediately obvious to him (Ferenczi, 1924 [264], *o.B. III*, p. 243).

---

*Ferenczi's writings are quoted by reference to the year of publication of the original; the figure in square brackets identifies the work in Balint's list of Ferenczi's writings (S. Ferenczi: *Bausteine zur Psychoanalyse*, Band IV. Bern & Stuttgart: Verlag Hans Huber, 1964).

Abbreviations:

B. = *Bausteine zur Psychanalyse* (Bern: Verlag Hans Huber, 1964).

FIR. = Ferenczi, *First Contributions to Psycho-Analysis* (London: Hogarth Press, 1955).

FUR. = Ferenczi, *Further Contributions to Psycho-Analysis* (London: Hogarth Press, 1955).

FIN. = Ferenczi, *Final Contributions to Psycho-Analysis* (London: Hogarth Press, 1955).

o. = original.

On this point, Freud and Ferenczi parted ways, Freud at times favouring the concept of *Einsicht,* the 'insight' of the Age of Enlightenment, while Ferenczi opted for *Erlebnisse,* or genuine experiences. But the history of the interaction between these two protagonists is much more complex. ...

NOTES

1. Besides, the title of one of his works on this subject is indeed: 'Recommendations to physicians practising psycho-Analysis' ('Rat-schläge') (1912e).
2. Freud's review of Edinger's 'Eine neue Theorie über die Ursachen einiger Nervenkrankheiten ...', has not been translated into English and is included neither in the *Standard Edition* nor in the *Gesammelte Werke.*
3. Statuettes of mummies, found abundantly in Egyptian tombs from the New Empire on [we are indebted to Professor Jean Rudhardt of the University of Geneva (Switzerland) for this information].
4. At times, Freud could be quite blunt in expressing his opinion of others. Blanton reports that Freud said of one of Ferenczi's pupils: 'She had, I'm afraid, a bad influence on Ferenczi', and of Dr. Karen Horney: 'She is able, but malicious—mean' (Blanton, 1971, p. 65).
5. Contrary to widespread belief, Freud alluded early in the century to analyses lasting from six months to three years rather than just a few weeks or months (Freud, 1904a, 7:254).
6. Kardiner adds: 'As with my father, I would repress my self-assertion with Freud in order to maintain his favor and support. The central fact in the transference situation was overlooked by the man who had discovered the very process of transference itself' (Kardiner, 1977, p. 100).
7. With the terms 'playground' and 'intermediary region', Freud alludes to concepts later developed by Ferenczi, Balint and Winnicott.

CHAPTER TWO

The enquiring Sándor Ferenczi

> I am ... regarded as a restless spirit ... a considerable
> majority ... have criticized the ... suggestions I have
> submitted. Freud ... did not mince matters ... But he
> hastened to add that the future might show me to have
> been right in many respects. ...
>
> Ferenczi (1931 [292], *FIN.*, pp. 126–127)

Before Freud's first technical papers were published,
Sándor Ferenczi* had noticed a fundamental
tendency manifest in the transference of the neurotic to include 'into the ego as large as possible a part of the
outer world' (Ferenczi, 1909 [67], *FIR.*, p. 47) and to merge
with the Other, which he associates with the avidity of drug
addicts. He outlined a transference relationship close to
that of hypnosis,[1] where the regressive aspect is linked to
insatiable emotional demands in the transference from the
start of treatment.

In a rapid, impressionistic style, full of enthusiasm and
very different from Freud's more balanced writing, Ferenczi
presents a wealth of perceptive, often unexpected, clinical
descriptions that illuminate everyday observations in a
surprising and original manner.[2]

Whereas Freud used dreams to explore the unconscious,
Ferenczi stressed their communicative value, as, for example, in his article 'To Whom Does One Relate One's

---

*Pronounciation: Shandor Ferentsi

19

Dreams?' (Ferenczi, 1913 [105], *FUR.*, pp. 349ff.). Having already perceived the analyst–analysand relationship in the light of his earlier experience with hypnosis (as in 1909 in 'Transference and Projection'), he went on to clarify the field of psychoanalysis. In two important articles published in 1919, 'Technical Difficulties in the Analysis of a Case of Hysteria' (Ferenczi, 1919 [210], *FUR.*, pp. 189ff.) and 'On the Technique of Psycho-Analysis' (Ferenczi, 1919 [216], *FUR.*, pp. 177ff.), he describes the intrusive nature of associations. In the second of the two, in the chapter on 'Control of the Counter-transference', he examines the analyst's responses, and, as Balint says in his introduction to the French Edition, 'every transference in the treatment situation is directed either toward *the indulgent mother* or *the stern father*' (Balint, 1966b, p. 153 [italics added]).

He links the transference experience to the patient's childhood situations and not to an abstract psychological framework.

Every patient is a kind of child and one of his greatest desires is to be treated as such by his analyst. ... In consequence, every analyst must learn how to graduate his sternness, indulgence, or sympathy, as the case may be. Expressed in different words, the analyst has a double task. On the one hand, he must listen sympathetically and accept everything that the patient offers to him, so as to be able to infer or reconstruct the patient's unconscious from the verbal material produced and from the patient's actual behavior; on the other hand, he must be in full control of his counter-transference (Balint, 1966b, p. 153).

The analyst is thus more and more at the centre of his thoughts.

C. Reverzy-Piguet speaks of 'the priority which Ferenczi assigns to experience. The care he took to avoid dogmatism and to preserve independent thought and freedom of action, made him suspicious of theoretical systems which he countered by stressing the importance and value of subjectivity and the justification of the error. It resulted in a method inseparable from clinical observation and experience. It is this position which provides his principal technical contributions' (Reverzy-Piguet, 1985, p. 9). What characterizes him is 'the desire to cure'. Sensitive to distress and suffering, Ferenczi always oriented his efforts towards care and healing—in other words, towards therapy. The theories and techniques he employed were constantly adapted to meet the particular needs of his patients, and most of them benefited from this consideration of his. To this may be added 'an intuitive awareness of the therapeutic potentialities of regression. This intuition grew out of his interest in the child, education and prevention. As a consequence, his research was oriented towards early trauma' (ibid.).

Ferenczi always considered that the analyst should be *active*. 'We are dealing ... with the formulation of a concept and technical term for something which ... has always *de facto* been in use but has never been named' (Ferenczi, 1921 [234], *FUR.*, p. 198). Examining his analytical activity as concretely as possible, Ferenczi thought he was only following Freud's suggestions, which called for active measures in the treatment of phobics and for imposing a time limit on therapy for certain cases of obsessional neurosis. He strove to clarify these procedures and their deeper significance and to *make explicit* what he and many Viennese analysts of that period did at times when analyses stagnated (cf. Fenichel, quoted in Lorand, 1966; Federn, 1933).

In his papers 'On the Technique of Psycho-Analysis' (Ferenczi, 1919 [216]) and 'Technical Difficulties in the Analysis of a Case of Hysteria' (Ferenczi, 1919 [210]), Ferenczi deals with the *resistances* that can attach to the rule of free association and free-floating attention. In these studies, he observes how rules themselves can be put to the service of resistances in the analysis. He suggests that the analyst may temporarily abandon so-called 'passive receptiveness' and exhort a patient to experience frustration[3] by, for instance, refraining from a particular gesture, for the purpose of bringing into the analysis tensions usually discharged through muscular activity.

In what are conventionally called his 'technical experiments', Ferenczi puts the analyst himself at the centre of his thinking and studies his attitude towards the patient from the alternating perspectives of the 'indulgent mother' or the 'stern father'. In the first phase of this research frustration was the main tool of 'active technique'. Later his imagination was increasingly captivated by the possibility of using gratification to promote cure. Anticipating that some would think he favoured 'coddling patients' (Ferenczi, 1930 [291], *FIN.*, p. 116), he pointed out that both frustration and gratification were already part and parcel of standard analytic practice. 'We do actually work with these two principles' (ibid.). However, since the two techniques had not been completely worked out, he felt that they should be stated explicitly so that analysts could determine more surely and easily when and how it would be appropriate to make use of them. 'Psycho-analysis demands of the physician untiring sensitivity to all of the patient's ideational associations, his emotions, and his unconscious processes. For this it is necessary that the physician himself have a flexible, supple mind. He can attain this only by being analysed himself' (Ferenczi, 1933 [293], *FIN.*, p. 153).

At the 1918 Budapest Congress Freud himself had questioned analytic technique as it then stood. Referring to Freud's example of adapting his own technique to the psychological make-up of his patients by settling a date for terminating the 'Wolf Man's' analysis and exhorting phobics to confront the surroundings they had previously avoided, Ferenczi questioned whether it was always reasonable for the analyst to remain passive or whether, on the contrary, he should not *vary* his attitude to suit the momentary context of the treatment. This question is the springboard for what has been called 'Ferenczi's experiments with technique'. These experiments developed out of the notion that in certain cases 'the flow of free association had become stagnant and unproductive as a result of the disappearance of libido from the actual analytical work for the sake of unconscious fantasies and unconscious bodily gratifications' (Balint, 1966b, p. 156). They were also based on the fact that an *active technique* might enable the analysand to resume the analytical work. The analyst could modify his attitude in such cases, particularly if he is in complete control of his counter-transference.

Among the more harmful attitudes in analysis is the authoritarian one. Ferenczi condemned it long before he had become interested in psychoanalysis (Lorin, 1983, passim) and was followed in this respect by Balint. 'The analyst's modesty must be ... a reflection of the limitations of our knowledge', he writes (Ferenczi, 1928 [283], *FIN.*, p. 94) and draws attention to 'the lofty attitude to the patient generally adopted by the omniscient and omnipotent doctor'. 'Analysis demands of the physician not only a firm control of his own narcissism, but also a sharp watch on his emotional reactions of every kind' (ibid., p. 95). 'One might say that [the analyst's] mind swings continuously between empathy,[4] self-observation and making judgments' (ibid., p. 96).

Ferenczi's concentration on understanding the analyst and *what he does* led him to envisage a 'metapsychology of the analyst's mental processes during the course of the analysis' (Ferenczi, 1928 [283], *FIN.*, p. 98)—that is to say, the study of all his personal cathexes, whether object-love, identifications, self-control or intellectual activity. Emphasizing the difficulty of this task, he wrote: 'During the long day's work [the analyst] can never allow himself the pleasure of giving his narcissism and egoism free play in reality' (ibid.). This article shows clearly that Ferenczi was aware of the far-reaching implications his investigations might have for psychoanalysis and of the need to proceed cautiously with them. 'Having regard to the great importance of any new technical recommendation, I could not make up my mind to publish this paper before submitting it to a colleague ... for criticism' (ibid., p. 99). He does not say who the colleague was, but we know from his correspondence that he was referring to Sigmund Freud (Grubrich-Simitis, 1986, p. 265). It is quite possible for this reason that he added:

I entirely share my critic's views that these technical precepts of mine, like all previous ones, will inevitably be misused and misunderstood, in spite of the most extreme care taken in drafting them. There is no doubt that many—and not only beginners, but all who have a tendency to exaggeration—will seize on what I have said about the importance of empathy to lay the chief emphasis in their handling of patients on the subjective factor, i.e. on intuition, and will disregard what I stated to be the all-important factor, the *conscious* assessment of the dynamic situation (Ferenczi, 1928 [283], *FIN.*, pp. 99–100 [italics in the original German text]).

In the same article he clearly describes the importance of 'empathy', of the subjective factor, as well as of detachment and conscious evaluation. He stresses these last two points: 'We try to follow the patient in all his moods, but we never cease to hold firm to the viewpoint dictated to us by analytic experience. My principal aim in writing this paper was to rob "tact" of its mystical character' (ibid.). While he claims to be in agreement with Freud, he cannot have been unaware that he was exploring uncharted territory: the possible uses of subjectivity and, above all, the *incorporation* of subjectivity into analytic thinking. Is it by chance that he concludes this article, one of his most significant works, by speaking of the analyst's 'combat' against 'that part of the superego which had become unconscious and was therefore beyond the range of influence ... ? [The analyst] will no longer have to obey his preconscious superego as slavishly as he had previously to obey his unconscious parent imago' (ibid., p. 101). It is easy to imagine that Ferenczi equated this superego with institutional regulations, and above all with the founder of the movement, towards whom Ferenczi maintained an analytical attitude, that is to say, by continuing to challenge ideas.

In actual fact Freud *acknowledged* the value of Ferenczi's work. It 'testifies to the pre-eminent maturity you have acquired during past years and which remains unequalled', he wrote, adding that his own 'recommendations on technique ... were essentially negative' (letter to Ferenczi dated 4 January 1928, in Grubrich-Simitis, 1986, p. 271).

Moreover, Ferenczi treated patients whose resistances could not be analysed by what he called 'classical technique' (circular letter dated 15 February 1924, in Freud, 1965a). He subsequently specified that for such patients, activity is only a prelude to interpretation (Ferenczi, 1926 [271], *FUR.*, pp. 217ff.), that the analyst must think with them in terms of transference neurosis, and the analytic process; he must encourage them to recognize the importance of mourning (Ferenczi, 1928 [282]), the effects of a 'not good enough' mothering (Ferenczi, 1929 [287]), the problems of abandonment, the narcissistic withdrawal (Ferenczi, 1931 [292]). He recognizes in them certain of those children who have matured too early and become the protectors of their own parents (Ferenczi, 1933 [294], *FIN.*, pp. 156ff.).[5]

In terms of process, he strove to define *the analyst's contribution* to the creation of an adequate psychological atmosphere (Ferenczi, 1930 [291], *FIN.*, p. 116). He establishes links between the personality, the analyst's personal style and the psychological atmosphere of the session. He shows how the frustrating active style increases the analysand's dependency on his analyst, how an authoritative attitude on the part of the analyst can contribute to the non-expression of affects and how a flexible style promotes the return of affects bound to unconscious infantile *traumas* that would remain inaccessible to any technique relying solely on the recall of accessible memories. Such observations imply that interpretations should always be presented to the patient as *tentative* formulations. He suggests that the work of interpretation might even be temporarily suspended during a state of regression. In this, he recognizes the place of regression in analysis (a theme subsequently developed by Michael

Balint) and its achievement by 'the technique of *play*' (Ferenczi, 1930 [291], *FIN.*, p. 121). 'In a conversation with Anna Freud in which we discussed certain points in my technique she made the following pertinent remark: "You really treat your patients as I treat the children whom I analyze". I had to admit that she was right' (ibid., p. 122).

Further on in the same article, Ferenczi acknowledges his indebtedness to his friend and colleague Groddeck. 'In making the two types of treatment more like one another I was undoubtedly influenced by what I saw of the work of George Groddeck' (ibid., p. 123). 'But, for my own part, I have remained faithful to the well-tried analytical method of frustration as well, and I try to attain my aim by the tactful and understanding application of *both* forms of technique' (ibid.). Thus, Ferenczi spoke as if there were *two techniques*—one that he termed 'classical' and another that he developed in his 'technical experiments'. It should be considered a possibility that if Ferenczi's views before and after 1926 were regarded as contradictory, it might be a function of experimentation, i.e. exploration in different directions. Moreover, the research underlying it was absolutely coherent: he was seeking to understand *the analyst's role* and its implications in the analytic process. Until then, the subject had been taboo. His intention was to determine the consequences of his different attitudes, of his verbal and non-verbal behaviour, the common ground on which analysis of himself and of his analysand meet. Such questions, cast up in the wake of these experiments, are still fundamental today. His writings thus 'made all analysts into his pupils' (Freud, 1933c, *22*:228). Or, as Michael Balint put it, 'Ferenczi's last writings not only anticipated the development of psycho-analytic technique and theory by fifteen to twenty years, but still contain many ideas that may shed light on problems of the present or even of the future' (Balint, 1958c, p. 68).

Ferenczi sensed that the analyst is in fact *inextricably implicated* in the analyses, and that the analysand must be able to perceive him as *dependable* (Ferenczi, 1928 [282],

FIN., p. 83). The patient makes 'an unconscious attempt ... to test the analyst's patience' and 'sharply observes the physician's reactions ... with great perspicacity'. He [the patient] detects 'the slightest sign of unconscious impulse in the [analyst], who has to submit to these attempts at analysis with inexhaustible patience; this often makes superhuman demands upon him which, however, are invariably worthwhile' (ibid.), especially with those patients, 'desperate cases', who unconsciously seek to be rejected (Ferenczi, 1928 [283], *FIN.*, p. 95). Ferenczi obviously felt that any other attitude—e.g. authoritarian or aloof—although easier on the analyst, would only convey the analyst's professional hypocrisy (Ferenczi, 1933 [294], *FIN.*, p. 158), a theme that had permeated his early writings (cf. Lorin, 1983). It was during a similar preoccupation towards the end of his life that he was faced with the need to guess the source of his own inner turmoil and to discuss it with the patient, admitting it perhaps not only as a possibility but as a fact (Ferenczi, 1933 [294], *FIN.*, p. 159). It is a question of 'mutual analysis'—analysis of the patient implies analysis of the analyst.[6] He brings up here the question of the existence and the extent of the *professional* as opposed to the unique and genuine personal relationship between the analyst and analysand.

Similar considerations were probably on his mind when he was thinking about the creation of the International Psychoanalytical Association. He said that he had recognized 'the pathology of such associations', and was 'aware that in most political, social and scientific organizations childish megalomania, vanity, admiration of empty formalities, blind obedience, or personal egoism prevail instead of quiet, honest work in the general interest' (Ferenczi, 1911 [79], *FIN.*, p. 302). His comments are lucid. He hopes that

The psycho-analytically trained are surely the best adapted to found an association which would combine the greatest possible personal liberty with the advantages of family organisation. It would be a family in which the father enjoyed no dogmatic authority, but only that to which he was entitled by reason of his abilities and labors. His pronouncements would not be followed blindly, as if they were divine revelations, but, like everything else, would be subject to thoroughgoing criticism, which he would accept, not with the absurd superiority of the pater familias, but with the attention that it deserved.

Recalling that it was on his initiative that the International Psychoanalytical Association was set up eighteen years earlier, he went on:

It groups all those who are interested in psychoanalysis and who do their best to preserve the purity of psychoanalysis according to Freud and develop it as a separate scientific discipline. On establishing this association I had decided in principle to admit as members only those people who adhered to the fundamental thesis of psychoanalysis [today, personal analysis is also a part of the entrance conditions]. I believed and I still believe that a productive discussion is only possible between people who think in the same way. Those who have adopted other basic principles as a starting point would do just as well in having their own centre of activity (Ferenczi, 1928 [306], o.B. III, p. 428).

He also said:

Though we analysts are now formally unorganized, we already live in a kind of family community, and in my opinion it would be right to give outward recognition to the fact (Ferenczi, 1911 [79], FIN., p. 303).

Ferenczi was well aware of the narcissistic gain of belonging to a group considering itself as avant-garde and the reassurance provided by its 'technique'. Thus, analysts can 'calmly allude to *superior knowledge* and erudite theories, seek and find the cause of the patient's failure, *instead of acknowledging their part [in it]*' (Ferenczi, 1985, p. 255 [italics added]).

Thus, brilliantly summing up his own course, Ferenczi demonstrates not only his sensitivity, but also the development of his viewpoint—his counter-transference.

Technique remained his main preoccupation throughout his life, or, as Balint said, it was his 'favorite topic' (Balint, 1966b, p. 147). Grubrich-Simitis points out that as early as 1916 in a letter to Freud, he wanted to concentrate only on 'subtleties of technique' (excerpt from a letter dated 14 August 1916, in Grubrich-Simitis, 1986, p. 260). Besides, Freud often encouraged him to do this. Some five years later he confirmed to Freud that he would 'seek better results with a more adequate technique' (excerpt from a letter dated 6 November 1921, ibid.).

The relationship between theory and technique is reflected in Ferenczi's preoccupation with trauma. The arguments advanced in his article 'The Unwelcome Child and His Death-Instinct' (1929 [287]) lead to those in 'Child Analysis in the Analysis of Adults' (1931 [292]) and in 'Confusion of Tongues between Adults and the Child' (1933 [294]), his last writings. He exposes the real traumas children may undergo in their relations with adults and insists on the necessity for the patient to relive those traumas emotionally in analysis, but not to repeat them there. As he conceives of the analytic experience, the patient's confidence in his analyst is an element of utmost importance. *'It is this confidence that establishes the contrast between the present and the unbearable traumatogenic past'* (1933 [294], *FIN.*, p. 160). He says that his patients have taught him 'to recognize and to control the exaggerations in both directions'—in other words, 'the aggressive features' of his 'active therapy', on the one hand, and 'the professional hypocrisy in the forcing of relaxation' (ibid.), on the other. 'Splitting' and 'friendly goodwill' are two key terms appearing in his writings dating from that period. What patients need is 'an atmosphere of confidence ... and ... full freedom' (1930 [291], *FIN.*, p. 118), and 'tenderness, not the violent ebullition of passion' (ibid., p. 121). All this leads to a 'new beginning' (1932 [308], *FIN.*, p. 271), a concept subsequently developed by others (Balint, 1968a, pp. 138ff.).

As we shall see, Ferenczi's final years were marked by his widening rift with Freud. Jones' (1955) biography of Freud, which until now has been the main source of information about their disagreement, focuses attention on Freud's letter of 13 December 1931. Jones publishes this letter *almost* in extenso. When Ferenczi had told Freud that one of his female patients (apparently Clara Thompson) was rewarded with a kiss at the end of each session, Freud is quoted as having replied,

> You have not concealed the fact that you kiss your patients and that you let them kiss you. ... There is none so revolutionary that he cannot find one more radical than himself. Some independent spirits, thinking about technique, might say to themselves: 'Why stop at a kiss?' Surely, one can go still further and include 'a hug', which, after all, will not get a woman pregnant. Still others, more daring, might go so far as to peep and to show, and soon we shall have accepted as an integral part of analytic technique all manner of petting parties and promiscuity. ... Our younger colleagues may find it difficult not to exceed the limits they had originally set for themselves. The godfather[7], Ferenczi, looking down upon the scene he had created, would say to himself: 'Perhaps, after all, I should have stopped *before* the kiss in working out my motherly love technique' (Torok, 1984, p. 96).

In his personal diary, Ferenczi reveals that Clara Thompson boasted: 'I can kiss Papa Ferenczi as often as I like' and that her statement was reported to Freud (Ferenczi, 1985, p. 45). In his own words, Ferenczi treated 'this distasteful incident' with 'total indifference'. Much later, Ferenczi became aware of the transferential implication of the patient's behaviour. 'As a child, her father ... had indulged in extensive sexual play with her ... and she sought revenge by "denouncing" him' (ibid., pp. 46–47).

Masson contends that it was not Ferenczi's experiments

with technique, but rather his ideas on childhood traumas that Freud found unacceptable (Masson, 1984, p. 166). In my opinion, the former element played a more important role. Probably, the most unbearable thing for Freud was the knowledge that Ferenczi had entered the 'ordeal' of severely regressed patients. This could hardly have failed to revive memories of his own early experiences of the Breuer period, Anna O., and, later (in 1908–1909), similarly difficult situations between Jung and Sabina Spielrein (1911–1912) and between Elma Palos and Sándor Ferenczi. The feature common to these situations was the very strong development of the erotic element in the relationship between patient and therapist. Freud was at first outside it, the 'third', in the role of observer; his involvement was sought only when difficulties arose. We shall come back to this. Freud aspired to create a situation comparable to a laboratory in order to satisfy his scientific ideals, as he conceived them, and the scientific nature of psychoanalysis, in particular that what is brought to the fore is not induced by the activities of the analyst. Freud felt that being overwhelmed by sexuality, regression and psychosis constituted a threat to this imago. At the heart of the problem we find the personal reactions of the two therapists, Freud and Ferenczi, to regressed patients. Remember that Freud did not like psychotic patients. Just how upsetting such experiences can be is clearly shown in a letter dated 21 November 1907, written by Breuer to Swiss psychiatrist Auguste Forel. Speaking of Anna O., Breuer writes: 'It was thus that I learned many things, things valuable from a scientific point of view, but also ... that it is impossible for a physician ... to treat such a case without having his practice and private life completely ruined by it. At the time, I swore *never again* to submit to such an ordeal' (quoted by Torok, 1984, p. 119). Freud must have had a similar experience: In the circular letter of 15 February 1924, he recalls his experiences and the fear they engendered, 'I value the joint book as a corrective of my view of the role of repetition or acting out in analysis. I used to be *apprehensive* of it, and regarded these incidents, or experiences as you now call them, as *undesirable failures*. Rank and Ferenczi now draw attention to the inevitability of these experiences and *the possibility of taking useful advantage of them'* (Freud, 1965a, p. 345 [italics added]).

But to return to Ferenczi, the divergencies did not lessen for all that. Although Ferenczi himself had reservations about what he was doing, he went ahead, and the gap widened. He was quite aware of what was happening. 'Freud's strong point is education, while mine is the technique of relaxation' (Ferenczi, 1985, p. 113). For him, Freud's views at the time were summed up by the following two statements: 'I cannot help but recall certain remarks Freud made in my presence, obviously relying on my discretion: "Patients are nothing but riffraff. The only useful purposes they serve are to help us earn a living and to provide learning material. In any case, we cannot help them"' (ibid., p. 148). 'I think that initially Freud sincerely believed in analysis; he followed Breuer with enthusiasm, and he devoted himself no less wholeheartedly to helping neurotic patients, if necessary lying on the floor for hours beside someone undergoing a hysterical fit. But he must have been first *shaken*, then *sobered* by certain experiences, just as Breuer had been when his patient relapsed and counter-transference suddenly opened up before him like an abyss' (ibid. [emphasis added]).

Apparently Ferenczi's experience with regressed patients enabled him to reach a better understanding of *traumas*:

1. In *all* cases where I have been able to penetrate deeply enough, I have discovered the hysterical *traumatic* underpinnings of the illness.
2. Where the patient and I have succeeded, the therapeutic effect has been greater. ...
3. The critical opinion which gradually developed in my mind during this time is that psychoanalysis *unilaterally practices* analyses of *obsessional neurosis* or character analyses, i.e. a psychology of the ego

while overlooking the organo-hysterical basis of the analysis; the cause resides in the *overestimation* of fantasy and the *underestimation* of the traumatic reality in the pathogenesis ...

4. Although they generally refer back to archaic experiences, newly acquired experiences also naturally have an impact on certain peculiarities of technique (Ferenczi, letter to Freud of 25 December 1929, quoted in Dupont, 1985, pp. 24–25).

Contrary to Masson (1984), I think that the overall problem of trauma and regression, and a psychoanalytic technique that makes it possible to experience a deep regression and to emerge from it through a 'new beginning', is what is truly at stake in the Freud–Ferenczi conflict.

Undoubtedly, when Freud spoke of 'boundless experimentation' (Freud, 1933a, 22:153), he was alluding to Ferenczi and warning those who would follow his lead: the analyst himself thus risks 'being forced away from analysis and drawn into a boundless course of experimentation' (ibid.). And yet, Freud declared after Ferenczi's death that 'It is impossible that the history of our Science will ever forget him' (Freud, 1933c, 22:229). Freud could have meant either that Ferenczi would be remembered *because of* his experiments or *in spite of* them.

Perhaps Balint comes closer to the truth when he writes that 'the disagreement between Freud and Ferenczi acted as a trauma on the analytical world' (Balint, 1968a, p. 152), and promoted a *silence* that suppressed this controversial issue. After Ferenczi's death, analysts were extremely circumspect in their discussions of technique, even though all subsequently admitted that the analysis of transference was a central issue. Problems of regression[8] and counter-transference seemed to disappear from discussions for a time—until Alice and Michael Balint published their 1939 article (Balint & Balint, 1939a).

In this chapter, I have endeavoured to underline those points that I consider important in understanding the controversy between Freud and Ferenczi. Such a controversy cannot, however, be detached from personal history, which I shall take up in the following chapter, in an 'intermezzo' devoted to the life of Ferenczi.

NOTES

1. In this article Ferenczi coined the word *introjection,* which he used more broadly than it has been used in the subsequent psychoanalytic literature.
2. Titles include: 'A Transient Symptom: The Position During Treatment' (Ferenczi, 1913 [115], *FUR.*, pp. 242ff.); 'On Falling Asleep During the Analysis' (Ferenczi, 1914 [139], *FUR.*, pp. 249ff.); 'Sensations of Giddiness at the End of the Psycho-analytic Session' (Ferenczi, 1914 [138], *FUR.*, pp. 239ff.).
3. Ferenczi does not use the terms 'frustration' or 'gratification' in this context. He frequently employs the word *Versagung* as noted by the French translators of his writings (Dupont, 1978, p. 12); they also established that Ferenczi uses this word in a wider sense than the one that is generally applied to it in psychoanalytic literature. Earlier on, we made the same remarks about 'introjection'. He does, indeed, have a particular way of using concepts so that they open possibilities for association to concepts that have yet to be created.
4. The original German text contains the corresponding word *Einfühlung.*
5. These personality types were recently re-investigated by Alice Miller (1979). Many recent 'discoveries', particularly during the past few decades, are contained and more clearly described in Ferenczi's publications. This may account for the present 'rediscovery' of his work.
6. Ferenczi's *Diary* bears witness to the fact that he recognized his patients' dependency needs and, moreover, their tendency to engage in reparation with their analyst—e.g., 'In R. N., I recognize the mother, the real one, who was hard and energetic and of whom I was afraid', he wrote, adding, 'R. N. knows it and treats me with exquisite tenderness' (Ferenczi, 1985, p. 94).
7. Sabourin (1982) draws attention (in his Preface to Volume IV of the French edition of *The Complete Works of Sándor Ferenczi*, p. 14) to Jones' mistakenly transcribing the term Freud had used, 'godfather', as 'God the Father'. If this is indeed the case, perhaps Jones was projecting his own megalomania onto Ferenczi.
8. 'By tacit consent, regression during analytic treatment was declared a dangerous symptom' (Balint, 1968a, p. 152).

CHAPTER THREE

Intermezzo:
Ferenczi—Biographical notes

> ... I had hoped you would outgrow that childish role and take your place beside me as an associate and a peer. You have not. ...
>
> Freud to Ferenczi in a letter dated 2 October 1910

Hungary's history had been enmeshed with Austria's for centuries. In 1526 the Hungarians, seeking protection against the expanding Turkish Empire, elected Ferdinand the First, head of the Eastern branch of the powerful Habsburg family, as their king. In 1723 Austrian Emperor Charles VI (King Charles III of Hungary), with no male offspring and wishing to ensure the continuing rule of the Empire by his lineage, issued a decree with the force of fundamental law, which overrode Salic tradition and guaranteed that his daughter Maria Theresa would succeed him on the throne. From that time onward, every ruler of the Austrian Empire was also ultimately crowned monarch over the Kingdom of Hungary.

After the 1848 revolt, the 'Compromise' ('between the House and the Nation') in 1867 and the constitution of the Dual Monarchy, Hungary gradually became a fairly liberal country in whose capital the population was composed of various traditions—a Catholic majority, and Protestant and Jewish minorities—and of different ethnic groups: Slavs, Germans and, naturally, Magyars. As in other countries, a gulf gradually developed between the capital and the rest of the country. Budapest evolved into a cosmopolitan city with a preponderant say in the affairs of the country, despite the opposition of the backward feudal provinces. During the final days of the monarchy and after its collapse towards the end of the First World War, a left-wing liberal party headed by Károlyi came to power in the autumn of 1918 and proclaimed a republic. In the spring of 1919, the veteran communist Béla Kun established a revolutionary government. This was followed several months later by the pre-fascist régime of Admiral Horthy, which developed later, for a decade, into a more moderate authoritarian government. The Social-Democratic Party was represented in Parliament, but the Communist Party was banned. A class of provincial gentry flourished in the shadow of Horthy and his military establishment, supported by a faction of the Catholic clergy whose opinions were clearly provincial, xenophobic and antisemitic. The rise of Fascism in Europe during the 1930s influenced Hungary as well. After Gömbös came into power in 1932, chauvinism was reinforced, as well as anticosmopolitanism and antisemitism.

The enthusiastic nationalism allied with hopes for progress that had flowered in 1848 deteriorated and, consequently, gave way to fierce provincial chauvinism and its twin, antisemitism, under the régime that took over the reigns of government after the destruction of the republic by Admiral Horthy in 1919.

Ferenczi is a typical representative of the fin-de-siècle intelligentsia of the capital, formed in 1872 by the reunification of Buda, the royal borough, and Pest, the city of tradesmen and craftsmen where the university was located. This intelligentsia, as far removed from provincial Hungary as the Parisian left bank from rural France, was composed of emigrés from all parts of the monarchy—the Germanic 'Schwaben', Jews from Western Poland (which had been part of the Dual Monarchy since the time of Maria Theresa) and Hungarians from distant provinces such as Transylvania, a multi-ethnic principality that had been independent for centuries and, with its minority of about two million Hungarian-speaking inhabitants, has since 1919 belonged to Rumania. In the nineteenth and at the beginning of the twentieth centuries, Vienna, Prague, Budapest and Trieste enjoyed an extraordinarily stimulating intellectual life, which produced geniuses such as Einstein, Kafka, Wittgenstein and Freud. Arthur Koestler vividly portrayed this cultural and scientific melting pot in his autobiographical novels *An Arrow in the Blue* (1952) and *The Invisible Writing* (1954). The fifty million inhabitants of this multinational empire, a prefiguration of a kind of Europe in miniature, at one and the same time conservative and avant-garde, liberal and antisemitic, spoke a score of languages without really understanding each other.

Budapest intellectuals displayed a typically Central European cosmopolitanism. Their number included the Marxist philosopher Georg Lukacs and Béla Balazs, the librettist for two well-known Bartok works ('The Wooden Prince' and 'Bluebeard's Castle'). Typically for their circle, Lukacs wrote most of his work in German, Balazs wrote German and Hungarian with equal ease, and Sándor Ferenczi kept his *private diary* in German![1] For those who have difficulty in imagining the cultural geography of these countries, it may seem surprising to see German cultural movements in cities like Prague or Budapest. But even the great Hungarian reformer of the early nineteenth century, Count Széchenyi, wrote in German. After all, isn't Yiddish, the spoken language of Jews in Poland and Russia, a German dialect?

Although the Empire finally crumbled under the pressure of nationalism, the cosmopolitan culture of the big cities of Central Europe profoundly marked our twentieth-century culture even after its downfall by expatriating its geniuses and talents: Freud to London, Wittgenstein to Cambridge, Schoenberg to California, among others.

After the Horthy regime came into power in 1919, the entire 'Spirit of Budapest' was challenged in the name of so-called 'Christian and national' values. Ferenczi and Hermann were among those persecuted. The inevitable consequence was a massive exodus of Hungarian intellectuals to Vienna, to Berlin, to the United States. At the beginning of the 1920s analysts such as Alexander and Harnik had left the country (Lorand had gone to New York, but most migrated to Berlin); during the 1930s Hungary's best physicists, such as Leo Szilard, musicians like Béla Bartok, and analysts like Robert Bak, Edith (Ludowyk) Gyömröi, David Rapaport, Géza Róheim, Sándor Feldman, René Spitz and others left the country in turn. Finally, after the Anschluss, John Rickman travelled from London to Budapest and, with his help, A. and M. Balint, among the last to leave the country, migrated to Great Britain.

The growing threat of Germany after the Austrian Anschluss (Vienna is only about 120 miles from Budapest) ended in the German occupation of Hungary in 1944. The country was liberated and occupied by the Soviet Army. The sovietization of Hungary, particularly after 1948, and the dismemberment of Eastern Europe (Koenigsberg, Kant's birth place, is now in the Soviet Union!) have placed the cities of Central Europe, once bastions of culture in the Empire—Prague, Lemberg, Budapest, Belgrade—into a cultural no-man's land. One of the last witnesses of that extraordinary flourishing of culture, Georg Lukacs, Marxist philosopher though he is, had to recant his ideas on many occasions, and finally the fire was extinguished.

This whole epoque is reflected in the family history and personal life of Sándor Ferenczi. His father, an immigrant Jew from Poland, born in 1830, the same year as Emperor Franz Joseph,[2] had enlisted in the Hungarian Army, an enthusiastic supporter of the 1848 Hungarian War for Independence. He had his German–Yiddish-sounding family name of Fraenkel 'magyarized'—legally changed—to the Hungarian Ferenczi out of enthusiasm for the liberal cause, rather than from a desire to forget his Jewish origins, to which he remained very attached. After the Hungarian insurrection had been defeated, he was demobilized and allowed to open a bookshop and publishing establishment in the provincial town of Miskolc, where he printed the political poems of the famous poet and Calvinist pastor Michael Tompa, and where many of his apprentices, such as George Fischer, founder of a well-known German publishing house, later became celebrated in their own right.

The eighth of twelve[3] children, Sándor was born in Miskolc in 1873. He grew up in a home rich with books and music, and already in his adolescence he wrote verses in the style of Heinrich Heine. He completed his secondary education at Miskolc and his medical studies at the University of Vienna.

He returned to Budapest in 1897, where he worked first at the St. Rókus hospital clinic for prostitutes. Then, in 1900, he entered the department of Neurology and Psychiatry in the St. Elisabeth Hospital, and in 1904 joined the Policlinic of a cooperative health insurance (Rajka, 1973). He then opened his own practice as general practitioner and neuro-psychiatrist and became a consultant psychiatrist for the judiciary. He left general medicine in 1910 in order to devote himself entirely to psychoanalysis.

Ferenczi had already experimented with hypnosis while still at school, and he read the 'Interpretation of Dreams' as a young doctor on the advice of his colleague and friend Fülöp Stein. It was at the beginning of 1908—when he was already 34 years old—that Stein organized a meeting with Freud for him. Freud 'was apparently so impressed by Ferenczi that he asked him to present a paper at the first Psychoanalytic Congress in Vienna in April 1908. Furthermore, he invited him to join the Freud family during the summer holidays at Berchtesgaden' (Balint, 1964g).

The following year he accompanied Freud to America. During their morning walks they discussed each of the five lectures Freud was to give at Clark University (Worcester, Mass.). A long friendship ensued, and during the First World War Freud did formal analysis twice with him (Balint, 1970f, p. 8; Grunberger, 1974, p. 528; Grubrich-

Figure 1. Freud and Ferenczi during their holidays in Austria, 1917.

Simitis, 1986, p. 260). Even Jones (Balint, 1964g, p. 10) who was not uncritical of Ferenczi, his analyst in 1913, writes that it is difficult to determine to whom should be attributed the profound thoughts and insights that germinated in the writings of Freud and Ferenczi during this period. In a letter to Ferenczi dated 11 January 1933, Freud writes: 'For many successive years we spent the autumn holidays together in Italy, and a number of papers that appeared later in the literature under his or my name took their first shape in our talks there' (Freud, 1933c). He described their relationship as having 'an intimate identity of experience, feelings and interests' (Grubrich-Simitis, 1986).

According to Balint, Ferenczi was the only analyst Freud ever invited to spend holidays together with him (Balint, 1964g). Ferenczi was privileged to discuss analytic problems with Freud—particularly transference and counter-transference problems and the analytic relationship. From their early acquaintanceship, Freud envisaged Ferenczi as his future son-in-law (ibid., p. 7), cherishing the idea of a marriage to his daughter Mathilde (Jones, 1955, pp. 61, 176). According to Jones, Ferenczi offered, in 1926, to come to Vienna to analyse Freud, and Freud was apparently touched by the offer (Jones, 1957, p. 120). Their long and very close relationship is reflected in a still unpublished correspondence, which dates from early 1908 to just shortly before Ferenczi's death on 22 May 1933. Together with the letters to Wilhelm Fliess (published in their entirety by Masson in 1985), the Freud–Ferenczi correspondence is certainly the most intimate Freud ever conducted with a friend and colleague. Overall, it represents a series of running commentaries on the practical and theoretical problems that arose during their lifetimes. It constitutes an invaluable treasury of information for a better understanding and critical evaluation of Freud's work. These letters supply the means of grasping every nuance of meaning, not only of related epistemological problems and of the nature of psychoanalytic conceptualization and knowledge, but also of the importance of personal factors, which are not to be overlooked in dealing with psychoanalytic practice. They also make it possible to study psychoanalytic controversies in depth (they deal amply with Adler, Jung, Rank, Reich) and the subsequent differences of opinion that developed between the two correspondents. This correspondence is a major contribution to the biographies of both Sigmund Freud and Sándor Ferenczi, to the better understanding of the lives of these two exceptional men and of the relationship between twentieth-century psychoanalytic thought and the cultural atmosphere of Vienna and Budapest. In this sense, it constitutes a document of our cultural history of the utmost importance.

As is to be expected in letters not intended for publication, their authors are less restrained in what they say and in how what they say is worded. They are spontaneous, sensitive, personal. They seem human in their faults and in their greatness.

Discretion and consideration for the privacy of still living persons have delayed publication of these documents for a certain time. However, it will not be long before they finally appear in print. A committee was formally constituted in 1985 in order to achieve this.

At the 1910 Nuremberg Congress, Freud prevailed on Ferenczi to propose the foundation of the International Psychoanalytical Association. In 1913 Ferenczi founded the Hungarian Psychoanalytical Society in Budapest, with Sándor Radó as Secretary, Istvan Hollos as Vice-president and Lajos Lévy as Treasurer. Among the first members of the Society were the literary critic Hugo Ignotus and the wealthy Budapest brewer Anton von Freund (later Freund-Tószeghy). 'Anton von Freund, perhaps the most lovable man in the early history of psychoanalysis, ... offered to put at the service of Freud's ideas a considerable sum ... and to organize an institute for (a) mass psychotherapy, (b) psychoanalytic training and (c) analytical research (but his) plans were shattered by events. ... inflation swallowed up the funds apart from a small sum for a [psychoanalytic] publishing house in Vienna. ... During the Hungarian revolution in 1919 an Institute was opened under Ferenczi's direction (in fact the first in the world), but a few months later the counter-revolution put an end to it' (Balint, 1948b, p. 168).

In 1914 Ferenczi was called up for military service as a doctor and assigned to duty at an army base in the little Hungarian garrison town of Pápa. Freud came to see him there once or twice, and Ferenczi often had occasion to travel to Vienna on leave. It was during this period that he underwent several stages of his analysis. At the end of the First World War, the Hungarian political climate changed radically: in October 1918, after the so-called 'Aster Revolution', 'Red Count' Károlyi formed a left-wing liberal government in coalition with the socialists. Under the new government, the faculty proposed in response to a student petition that Ferenczi be named professor of psychoanalysis at the university (the first time a chair of psychoanalysis had been created by any university). Géza Róheim was appointed professor of anthropology, and Géza Révész[4] professor of medical psychology.

When Béla Kun's communist government came to power, Ferenczi's appointment was confirmed in 1919 by Zsigmond Kunfi, Commissar of Labor and Public Welfare. For this reason, it was immediately rescinded when Horthy seized power.

Ferenczi fell in love with Gizella Palos (1863–1949), née Altschul, probably during 1904. Then, in 1911, he told Freud that he had become infatuated with Elma, her daughter, who was in analysis with him for a depression following the suicide of her friend. 'I could not maintain the cold superiority of the analyst with Elma', he confessed (letter to Freud, 3 December 1911) and, at the end of that year, even mentioned the possibility of marriage. ...

So he found himself in a veritable triangle between his mistress and the young woman, his patient, and, even worse, tormented by doubts: it was a matter of 'marriage or treatment of the sickness' (letter to Freud, 1 January 1912). In that same letter Ferenczi requested most urgently that

Freud take over the analysis of the young woman who had become his fiancée. 'Since you require neither my inclinations nor my predictions but you *require* [underlined in the original] me to take her into analysis, I am obliged to do so. Although in principle I have no free hour. ...' (letter from Freud to Ferenczi, 2 January 1912). There followed a period of insecurity, of changes of decisions, although Ferenczi was aware that in rushing headlong into the affair he came close to realizing his own family story and, at the end of the day, became 'a modest man' (letter to Freud, 3 January 1912). There was an exchange of the utmost intimacy between them, with Freud revealing quite openly the most personal details of what he had learned from his analysand. Ferenczi gradually distanced himself and spoke of the 'mishap' that had led him to lose control of his 'mastery of oneself' (letter, 20 January 1912). After Elma had completed a 'piece of analysis' with Freud between the New Year and Easter 1912, Ferenczi took her back to finish the analysis, in understandably very difficult circumstances, and with the same courage he was to show each time he had to admit that he had made a mistake. There remained in him a sadness to which he did not find resignation easy and which perhaps was never entirely accomplished.

This aspect of Ferenczi's personal life is of great significance, all the more as Freud played a part in it.[5] In a letter dated 27 February 1922 Ferenczi writes: 'Professor Freud has taken an hour or so to deal with my problems. He holds fast to the opinion he expressed previously, i.e. that my main hang-up is the hostility I bear *him* because (just as my father did before him) he prevented my marriage with the younger of my fiancées (now, my step-daughter). And for this reason my murderous thoughts toward him ...' (Ferenczi & Groddeck, 1982, p. 64).[6] However that may be, he could marry Gizella in 1919, on the same day that Gizella's ex-husband Palos died of a heart attack (Dupont, 1982, p. 35).

At the Budapest Congress in September of 1918 Ferenczi was elected President of the International Psychoanalytical

Association (Balint, 1949a). Because of Hungary's political isolation and the precariousness of communications with Hungary (especially the disruption of postal services), Ferenczi judged it advisable, a few months later, to resign this position.

The Budapest Congress, Freud's presence in Hungary, Ferenczi's election to the Presidency of the International Association, coincided with the peak of his friendship with Freud. In 1914 Freud had written: 'Hungary, so near geographically to Austria, and so far from it scientifically, has produced only one collaborator, S. Ferenczi, but one who is himself worth a society' (Freud, 1914d, 14:33). By 1918, however, he had begun to make plans to turn Budapest into the headquarters of the psychoanalytical movement (Freud, 1965a, p. 278). Indeed, the Hungarian culture of this epoch seems to have been fertile ground for implanting psychoanalysis. The atmosphere was perhaps less favourable to highly abstract thought such as philosophy, and more propitious to fields such as music, painting and —thanks to its ties with the Viennese School—medicine. The budding Hungarian psychoanalytical school was quite independently minded—for instance, in its training system—less beholden to authority (which brought it into conflict with the Berlin Institute, where training was straight off organized and systematized, and thinking structured).

Ferenczi was the uncontested leader of the first circle of psychoanalysts in Budapest. This circle included such personalities as Hollós, probably one of the first psychiatrists to use psychoanalysis to understand psychosis and, with this view, to liberalize insane asyla.[7] Hollós probably influenced Professor Moravcsik, who held the chair of Psychiatry in Budapest, to write, already in 1913, an article recognizing the importance of Freud's researches. In 1926 Hollós published a novel about life in a sanatorium, as seen through the eyes of a psychoanalyst. It was a bestseller in the 1930s and has been translated into French by J. Dupont as 'Mes Adieux à la maison jaune' [Farewell to the yellow

house] (Editions Coq-Héron, Paris). He became President of
the Hungarian Psychoanalytical Society after Ferenczi's
death in 1933. There was also Kata Lévy, the child analyst
and sister of Anton von Freund-Tószeghy, and her husband
Lajos Lévy, who later became Ferenczi's personal physician.
Lévy was keenly interested in psychoanalysis of the early
myths in the Bible. A widely circulated anecdote attributes
a gruesome slip of the tongue to him: as Ferenczi lay bed-
ridden and seriously ill, he is reported to have told him
that the medicine he was prescribing for him was 'as sure as
death'.

By the end of the 1930s Imre and Alice Hermann were to
become the leaders of the group and to remain so until
Imre's death in 1984 at the age of 94. He is the originator of
the concept of the clinging instinct, inspired by his
observations of primates in the 1930s (Hermann, 1933,
1943). His description of clinging and of investigative
behaviour (Hermann, 1936) undoubtedly inspired Balint in
his development of the concepts of ocnophilia and philobatism. Sandor Rado, Jenö Harnik, Franz Alexander (son of
Bernard Alexander, an exceptionally cultured professor of
philosophy) also belonged to the Society. All emigrated to
Berlin in the early 1920s. Alexander was later to become
head of a Chicago group interested primarily in psychosomatic medicine and problems of psychoanalytical technique. This group included Theresa Benedek and Thomas
Szasz, also known for their work on the problems of
psychoanalytic training, and in the next generation John
Gedo, whose thinking has mainly dealt with questions of
practice and technique. All three display the independence
of thought and non-conformity characteristic of the
Budapest School. Sandor Rado went to live in New York,
where he founded the Psychoanalytic Society and Institute at Columbia University. Sándor Feldman emigrated
directly to the United States and Edith (Ludowyk-) Gyömröi
to Ceylon, and from there to London. She was the analyst of
one of Hungary's greatest poets, Attila Jozsef. Lilla
Veszy-Wagner, also established in London, compiled the

index to the *Gesammelte Werke,* the German edition of Freud's *Complete Works* commissioned by Imago and finally published by Fischer. It was a mammoth task in those computerless times, and she lived for years surrounded by thousands of slips of paper and index cards! Lajos Székely had already gone to Sweden in 1930. Robert Bak, who also cared for Attila Jozsef, emigrated to New York. David Rapaport became an analyst only after his emigration, first to Israel in 1939, then to the United States. Sándor Lorand practised mainly in the United States. Lilly Hajdu, a psychiatrist, endeavoured, mainly after the Second World War, to contribute to the liberalization of asyla. Her son was executed after the revolutionary events of 1956, and when she was informed, much later, of his death, she committed suicide.

Géza Róheim, anthropologist and psychoanalyst, emigrated to New York. According to statistics, he is, together with Georg Lukacs, among the Hungarian-born authors most widely read in the West.

Endre Almássy, president of the group that remained in Budapest, did his best to maintain decent living and working conditions for the group during the 'brown years' of Nazi persecution and to save what could be saved. Despite his efforts, the tragedy could not be avoided: six of the twenty-six members and two of the eleven candidates fell victims to Nazism (Nemes, 1985).[8]

What characterized the Budapest group was its informality. Ferenczi met regularly in cafés like the Café Royal on the Grand Boulevard with a circle of friends composed of eminent artists and writers. His friendship with Frederick Karinthy, famous writer and humorist, and with Hugo Ignotus, literary critic, author, poet and columnist, is reflected in his writings (Ferenczi, 1924 [266][9] and [267][9]).

Dezsö Kosztolányi, the well-known poet and satirist, and Sándor Hevesi, the playwright, stage manager and future director of the Hungarian National Theater, also belonged to this circle. It was with reference to this period that Ferenczi later wrote: 'Where are those carefree, pre-war days under Franz Joseph, when a line of poetry, a witty turn of phrase, a scientific discovery, could stir the very souls of men?' (Ferenczi, 1924 [267][9]).

The intelligentsia gathered in various circles, the most prestigious of which were the Society for Social Sciences, founded in 1901 with its review 'Huszadik Század' [The Twentieth Century], and the Galileo Circle, a society of antimilitarist free-thinkers, formed in 1908, the same year that Hugo Ignotus and his friends Ernö Osvát and Max Fenyö began publishing the avant-garde literary review 'Nyugat' [The West]. To this movement belonged Dezsö Kosztolányi and Georg Lukacs (who was close to Kierkegaard, Simmel and Stefan George), the great Hungarian poet Endre Ady, the musicians Béla Bartok and Zoltan Kodaly ... and Ferenczi (Ignotus, 1972, p. 125).

In another group consituted in 1915 and known as 'The Sunday Circle', we find several of the same people, but also Béla Balazs, Karoly Mannheim, known first in Frankfurt am Main and later in London as a sociologist, Antal Frigyes, author of the famous *Florentine Painting and Its Social Background*, Charles de Tolnay, future director of the Casa Buonarotti in Florence, Jenö Varga, future Soviet economist, Mihaly Polanyi, scientist in Great Britain, and, among the psychoanalysts, René A. Spitz and Edith Ludowyk-Gyömröi (Karadi & Vezer, 1980). This intermingling of psychoanalysis with progressive cultural movements was more characteristic of Budapest than of other early psychoanalytic centres, a phenomenon undoubtedly linked to Ferenczi's personality.

After the downfall of the Empire at the end of the War, Ferenczi was a victim of persecution under the 'White Terror' of the Horthy régime because of his ideas, incompatible with the then dominant military–clerical conservatism, and because of his Jewish background. After the 'crane-plumed' officers referred to by Hermann in his memoirs (1975) had come to power and even during the consolidation of the Horthy régime, Ferenczi endured hardship for many long years. He was forced to resign from the Hungarian Medical Society. For the next ten years, he became more and more withdrawn, confining himself to his consulting room and devoting his activity to psychoanalytic research, mainly on technical problems.

Several of his early collaborators and friends left the country, as we have already said; some (Rado, Alexander, Harnik, Klein[10] and others) went to Berlin, at the time an attractive capital and the crossroads of a wide variety of cultural movements. Ferenczi suffered deeply from a feeling of isolation. 'It is tragic', he wrote in 1923, 'when, after fifty years of thinking and feeling at home in one's own native land, one's right to belong to the national community is challenged' (Ferenczi & Groddeck, 1982, p. 109). When on his deathbed he wrote to Freud, beseeching him to seek refuge abroad, Ferenczi was a step ahead in experience. For a long time he had been unsure whether to leave Hungary, thinking first of going to Berlin (Eitingon, 1933, p. 295).

In fact, he was more attracted to the idea of working in America, like Otto Rank. He imagined that once he had established a reputation there through lectures and supervisions, he could take American patients paying in dollars in Budapest—as Rank did in Paris—and that there might even be an opportunity to transfer his work to the United States, as Rank was to do in 1935, after a decade of commuting between Paris and New York. Freud, however, did not want to 'lose' his favourite colleague and friend for the sake of America, for what he called 'the barbarous Dollaria' (letters from Freud to Ferenczi of 18 September 1926 and 8 August 1927). Moreover, generally speaking, he did not like to see his pupils emigrate to the United States. He felt rather sentimental about such departures, regarding them as signs of infidelity. Indeed, as far as Rank was concerned, it was a way of putting some distance between himself and the Master. So Ferenczi wrote in 1926: 'I have submitted to powerful influences which wanted me to give up the trip to America and move instead to Vienna to take up the presidency. Professor Freud was very strongly *for* Vienna and *against* "America"' (Ferenczi & Groddeck, 1982, p. 102 [italics in the original]).

These events are inseparable from the crisis that began after the publication, in 1924, of *The Development of Psychoanalysis* written by Ferenczi and Rank. Freud's first reaction was a rather favourable one ('Its discovery is magnificent', letter from Freud to Ferenczi, 1 June 1923), but after the appearance, in the same year, of a second work by Rank on *The Birth Trauma*, when the two books became objects of criticism in psychoanalytic circles, Freud distanced himself ('The book would not have been written if he [Rank] had been analyzed', letter from Freud to Ferenczi of 29 August 1924). Eventually, in loyalty to Freud and after a period of trying to act as intermediary, Ferenczi, too, separated from Rank. Between Freud and Rank there ensued a long and painful series of arguments, reunions and separations resembling a divorce process with everyone trying to avoid a violent rupture.

Ferenczi made up his mind to spend some time in America in response to an invitation from the New School for Social Research in New York to give lectures on psychoanalysis. He stayed there, with his wife, for eight months from the autumn of 1926. In accordance with his hopes, he encountered a great deal of interest in his activities as analyst and supervisor. The visit was not, however, without tension because of the disagreement among the majority of the New York Society membership (curiously, supported by Ernest Jones) over the psychoanalytic training of non-medical candidates, which both Freud and Ferenczi considered desirable.

Sándor Ferenczi returned to Budapest in the following spring, resumed his activities and, three years later, in 1930, founded the Psychoanalytic Policlinic, later directed by Michael Balint.

*   *   *

Having arrived at the point in Ferenczi's life that was

marked by the difficulties in his relationship with Freud, we need to consider why it became such a tragic turn of events for him. Probably the key to this is in a letter to Groddeck written on Christmas Day 1921. 'What I wanted was to be loved by Freud' (Ferenczi & Groddeck, 1982, p. 57). It is easy to be led astray by conjecture about Ferenczi's analysis with Freud;[11] its reconstruction is a hazardous venture, even with the help of his correspondence with Freud, which does, however, provide some clues.[12] The rift with this man who was his analyst, his friend, and his senior, caused Ferenczi great suffering, the more so as he always considered Freud a genius. In a letter to the Groddecks dated 20 March 1933 he wrote, 'I am feeling down not only through sheer physical exhaustion but also because of disappointment regarding Freud' (ibid., p. 127).

Although Ferenczi sought new ways to understand the analytic situation, he was nevertheless very much attached to the collaboration with his analytic colleagues, to the analytic community and to the International Psychoanalytical Association that he had helped to found. Sensitive as he was, to feel excluded, rejected, refused and misunderstood was a catastrophe for him. Masson thinks that Ferenczi acted as if he were saying to Freud, 'I will not be part of [your movement]' (Masson, 1984, p. 186). But in reality, he *wanted to belong* to it, and he felt he had every right to do so. He wanted Freud to acknowledge and accept his views. When the first signs of disagreement were in the air, he declared vehemently: 'I consider your fear that I will develop into a second Stekel to be unfounded' (letter dated 27 December 1931; ibid., p. 160). He fretted over the slightest difference of opinion with Freud. In his letters he is constantly seeking reassurance that Freud thinks like him, and anxious not to risk offending Freud by surpassing him. In a letter to Freud written in 1930 he criticizes him for not having been aware of his, Ferenczi's, negative feelings towards him, his analyst. Freud's reply, seven years later, is well known and appears in 'Analysis Terminable and Interminable' (Freud, 1937c, 23:221); he explained that it was not possible to analyse negative transference that did not crop up spontaneously during analysis. One feels the dissatisfaction and conflictiveness of their complex analytical and personal interactions through Ferenczi's letters to Groddeck. 'Never before', he wrote in 1921, 'have I spoken so openly to any man, not even to "Sigmund" ... At times, I let him analyze me (once for three weeks, another time for four or five weeks). For years we spent our holidays together, (but) I was unable to open up completely to him. ... He overawed me, he was too much of a father figure' (letter dated Christmas Day of 1921, in Ferenczi & Groddeck, 1982, p. 56). How right he was when he wrote to Freud 'Our relationship is made up ... of a tangle of conflicting opinions and emotions' (letter of 17 January 1930, in Dupont, 1985, p. 25).

As time passed, however, the conflicts were expressed more and more in actions. Grunberger quotes the book written by the writer Zsófia Dénes, niece of Ferenczi's wife: 'Having been shown in to the house by Ferenczi to see Freud ... she was struck by Freud's excessive coldness compared with the first visit and she could not fail to conclude that something important had happened in the relationship between the two men. Whereas Ferenczi had been one of the family and Freud had called him "my dear son", this time Ferenczi was obliged to have himself announced, was briefly received and quickly dismissed. Only Gizella was given a friendly smile and it was she who, on leaving, burst into tears'. Further on, Grunberger writes: 'According to the witnesses—Zsófia Dénes, Izette de Forest and Erich Fromm—when Ferenczi once communicated his new views on psychoanalysis to Freud in Semmering where Freud was spending his summer vacation, the Professor listened impatiently, made a few caustic remarks, and when Ferenczi held out his hand to take leave, Freud abruptly turned on his heels and left the room' (Grunberger, 1974).

Despite these incidents, in 1932 Freud again asked Ferenczi about the presidency of the International Psychoanalytical Association. The wording of his offer made

Figure 2. Sándor Ferenczi (photograph).

it sound as if he were trying to make it a therapeutic aim. Indeed, in his letter of 12 May, he expressed concern: 'These past few years you have withdrawn into isolation. ... You should leave that island of dreams where you live with the offsprings of your imagination and rejoin the fray' (Dupont, 1985, p. 28). But Ferenczi chose to remain with the 'offsprings of his imagination', to survey the landscape of his fantasies rather than to 'rejoin the fray', the pathology and vanity of which he had clearly come to recognize. 'I truly believe I can accomplish something useful by pursuing my present mode of work' (ibid.).

Ferenczi's withdrawal caused gossip. It was whispered that he was 'not well, not himself'. His neurological condition was incurable at the time. He suffered from pernicious anaemia, which today can be cured with Vitamin

B_{12}. Damage to the central nervous system, however, had progressed to a point where it was irreversible. He died on 22 May 1933.

Jones echoed the rumour that Ferenczi had lost his mind (Jones, 1957, pp. 176, 178). In the subsequent disagreement between him and Balint, Jones alluded to an unidentified 'witness' who had alleged that Ferenczi's mind had been affected, contrary to accounts given by many qualified physicians and psychiatrists who saw Ferenczi in person just prior to his death (Balint, 1958c; Lorand, 1966; Hermann, 1975). The awareness of his fatal illness, his disagreements with Freud, the difficulties he experienced on the path of analysis, were each ordeals in their own right and must have caused him great anguish. But there is a big difference between personal anguish and madness. Ferenczi presented classical clinical signs of funicular myelosis as a result of his pernicious anaemia. There is no doubt about this diagnosis, and any other interpretation is but a sad story.

One might reflect on some of the rather strange expressions in Freud's correspondence with Ferenczi in order to throw some light on them. They do make one wonder. For instance, the term 'Grand Vizir' (letter, 13 December 1929, in Jones, 1957, p. 147). For a Viennese, such a term—being a reference to the *Turks* who for 400 years represented the neighbouring dangerous *enemy* and, in part, the occupier—cannot but have negative connotations.

To quote another example, in a letter to Ferenczi, dated 4 February 1924, Freud uses the old word—ambiguous in this context—of *Handlungsreisende,* which sounds similar to *(Be)handlung* [treatment]. The word 'act (out)' corresponds to *handeln. Handlungsreisende* means 'commercial traveller' but also a traveller who *acts* (out). The term appears already in 1912 in the Freud–Ferenczi correspondence in reference to Jung. This fact, that the term had been applied to Jung before Ferenczi, must have had an ominous bearing on him. After several misunderstandings during the first holidays they spent together in Palermo, Freud wrote to him: 'I am [not] the psychoanalytic "superman" that we have created and I have not got the better of the counter-transference' (10 October 1970). Freud, however, forgot the 'not' in the first part of the sentence ('*ich bin auch jener psa. Uebermensch den wir konstruiert haben*'), which gives exactly the opposite meaning and may well show Freud's ambiguity with respect to his own wishes in this relationship.

Such ambiguities of meaning should be seen in relation to the phenomenon Freud speaks of in 'The Interpretation of Dreams', when he writes with great frankness: 'Having an intimate friend and a hated enemy were always an indispensable part of my affective life; I have always been able to acquire the one and the other, and it was not unusual for the friend and the enemy to be one and the same person' (Freud, 1900a, 5:483).

It was thus in an atmosphere of conflict, sometimes sadness, wounded narcissism and hurt feelings that the most crucial questions in psychoanalytic technique germinated. The future will not be very different; it is already casting its shadow.

Many have expatiated on the rift between Freud and Ferenczi, as well as over the rivalry between Jones and Ferenczi. It has become commonplace to attribute the latter to the unresolved transference relationship from Jones' 1913 analysis with Ferenczi. Strachey and Glover thought that Jones 'could never forgive Ferenczi for having been his analyst' (Roazen, 1975, p. 358). Moreover, Jones had access to the Freud–Ferenczi correspondence while he was writing his biography of Freud; it is easy to imagine that the remarks about him in this correspondence did nothing to increase his affection for Ferenczi,[13] although it apparently in no way affected his idealization of Freud. Some of the errors committed by Jones in this biography—especially the way he represented Ferenczi—have since been rectified. Nevertheless, 'publication of Jones' biography resulted in a flood of written acrimony' (Balint, 1985 [1969i], p. 14).

Figure 3. Sándor Ferenczi (painting, 1923, by O. Dormandi [-Székely-Kovacs]).

Survivors of that epoch who knew Ferenczi almost unanimously testify to his warmth, intelligence, wit and imagination. Wrinkles invariably dissolve into smiles when they are asked to recall him. He was much loved by his colleagues. In his obituary, Max Eitingon spoke of Ferenczi's great popularity and exceptional lovableness, which made him the most appreciated among his colleagues, after Freud himself. He writes: 'I liked Ferenczi above all for his devotion to our profession and then for his profound kindness' (Eitingon, 1933, p. 290).

Ferenczi was reputed to be a brilliant therapist. Sterba even wanted to send his friend Wilhelm Reich to him to be reanalysed! (Sterba, 1982, p. 88). Sterba also reports Helene Deutsch's opinion that Ferenczi 'could even cure a horse' (a not entirely unambivalent metaphor, as *Rosskur* in German has the same connotation of astringent treatment as 'horse medicine' does in English). Was this a reference perhaps to the regression he allowed, or an allusion to his 1913 article 'Taming of a Wild Horse' (Ferenczi, 1913 [104], *FIN.*, pp. 336–340)?

The entire life of this so sensitive and somewhat vulnerable man was full of conflict and tension, both privately and professionally. He had to wait many years before marrying his mistress. From the end of 1919, long before the rise of Nazism in Central Europe, he suffered political persecution, which affected his professional activity, and, together with Freud, he was deeply involved in the controversy over lay analysis, which both men favoured.

Some correspondence dating from Ferenczi's lifetime contains evident signs of tensions between Karl Abraham and Ferenczi, between the Zurich and the Berlin school on the one side and the Budapest school on the other. Ferenczi criticized the Berlin school for its lack of interest in technique and its overemphasis on theory. Perhaps this promoted the antagonism between Ferenczi and Abraham, but by their very natures they were unlikely to have been in accord—the one lively, curious, intuitive and roguish; the other, an organizer, a rigorously scientific thinker considered by some to be rigid.

It would be interesting to know whether Melanie Klein's few references to Ferenczi during her London years may have been the consequence of her stay in Berlin. No doubt, however, her attitude regarding the analysis of transference and her interest in children was decidedly influenced by him. One author notes interestingly that 'whether they agree or disagree on theory, both Melanie Klein and Ernest

Jones betray their common filiation to Ferenczi' (Girard, 1983, p. 1190).

It was Ferenczi's fate: he could not be easily fitted into any preconceived pattern. He was too alive, too sensitive, and much too ready to respond. He was always willing to experiment with new responses until one of them led him to a new idea or to a new insight. True, the new idea in some cases had to be modified or qualified by further experiences, but much more often than not it was revealing, stimulating and—this was also part of Ferenczi's fate—it very often upset something in which other people still firmly believed, bestowing upon him the doubtful reputation of an iconoclast, the *enfant terrible* of psychoanalysis' (Balint, 1966b, pp. 148–149 [italics in the original]).

Enfant terrible or 'wise baby',[14] he was at any rate far removed from 'adult' hypocrisies, and in touch with the child in the adult ... and his problems.

NOTES

1. When Béla Bartok arrived in Budapest to study at the Franz Liszt Academy of Music, most of the instruction was given in German. This was no problem for Bartok, who had attended a secondary school in Bistricz/Beszterce, Transylvania (then part of Hungary), at which all subjects were taught in *German* (Szegö 1964, p. 42).
2. In English also Francis Joseph.
3. A daughter died when Ferenczi was five years old. This is probably why some biographies refer to eleven children (Dupont, 1982, p. 28).
4. Although not an analyst, Révész was very close to the analytic circles: his wife was Franz Alexander's sister, and his own sister was married to Sándor Rado; Imre Hermann was assistant in his Budapest laboratory. After 1919 he emigrated to Holland and became professor at the University of Amsterdam.
5. Speaking of his wife, Ferenczi later wrote to Groddeck: 'I have again spoken to her of dissatisfaction, of repressed love for her daughter (who should have been my fiancée, which, incidentally, she was until Freud made a rather disapproving remark which led me to take a firm

stand against that love and openly reject the young lady)' (Ferenczi & Groddeck, 1982, p. 58).

6. Conceivably, Ferenczi's obsessive fear that he would quarrel with Freud originated in his (unconscious) hostility towards his analyst.

7. Freud was unreceptive to Hollós's ideas. In a letter, Freud writes: 'I did not like those patients ... an astonishing intolerance which brands me a poor psychiatrist ... could my attitude result from an increasingly firm stance in favor of the intellect, the expression of my hostility toward the "Id"?' (Sabourin, 1985, p. 167).

8. According to a census in 1941, the Jewish community had 725,000 members, 440,000 of whom were deported to Auschwitz during the German occupation, between May and July 1944; only 250,000 survived (Braham, 1981, p. 143).

9. Not included in the approved English edition of Ferenczi's complete works.

10. Melanie Klein resided in Budapest from 1911 to 1919, migrated to Berlin in 1921, then to London in 1926. Grosskurth remarks that although Melanie Klein more often refers to Abraham in her theoretical works, she had more to say about Ferenczi in her autobiographical notes where she said that she was 'delighted to be together with a man of unusual gift'. She adds: 'he had a touch of genius' (Grosskurth, 1986).

11. Whatever the ingenuity (real or imagined) of some analysts, it must be admitted that it is very difficult to reconstruct those analyses in which we participate either as analysand or analyst.

12. The, as yet, unpublished correspondence between Freud and Ferenczi is currently housed in the Austrian National Library in Vienna (see also Introduction, page xvii).

13. In addition, Ferenczi accused Jones of plagiarism in one of the Committee's circular letters (Grotjahn, 1976, p. 113).

14. Ferenczi uses this English term in his original German texts. [See, for instance, the article 'Exaggerated Sex Impulse und seine Folgen', in o.B. IV, p. 285; no English translation].

CHAPTER FOUR

Psychoanalytic practice in the 1920s and 1930s

> It might be expected that of all the subjects with which
> psychoanalytic literature deals, questions involving
> *what actually takes place* in a psychoanalytic treatment
> and *how the analyst's part* therein may be made most
> effective would predominate. But this expectation does
> not prove to be correct.
>
> Otto Fenichel, 1941

The discovery that free association is hampered by internal resistances radically altered the way in which psychoanalysts explored the unconscious. Although Freud had initially looked on resistance as nothing but an obstacle (Freud, 1913c, *12*:143–144), he had changed his mind completely on this score by 1923, when he wrote that it was a factor 'scarcely to be over-estimated in the dynamics of the process of cure' (Freud, 1923a, *18*:247). In 1913 he had already written: 'So long as the patient's communications and ideas run on without any obstruction, the theme of transference should be left untouched. One must wait until the transference, which is the most delicate of all procedures, has become a resistance' (Freud, 1913c, *12*:139).[1] It was only later that he thought that it was precisely the transference that made systematic work on the unconscious a possibility. 'This transference alike in its positive and in its negative form is used as a weapon by the resistance; but in the hands of the physician it becomes the most powerful therapeutic instrument' (Freud, 1923a, *18*:247). Transference, particularly when it is interpreted as

61

resistance, can be used as a tool for pursuing the original aims of psychoanalysis: to liberate the *repressed,* to *render conscious* the *unconscious.*

Broadly speaking, the aim of psychoanalytic theory is to define the content or nature of the unconscious and to apprehend its scope. Practice raises other questions: what is the analyst's role in the interpretation of transference? To what extent should it be systematically interpreted? How best can it be understood? Analysts addressed these issues in several ways. Some scrutinized their own perceptions, their own internal life, which was mobilized by the treatment—in other words, they tried to understand the transference through the counter-transference, as Ferenczi did. Glover (1924) and later Sterba (1936) took a similar approach. Still others, putting into practice Freud's 1913 admonition to leave the transference untouched until it had become a resistance, endeavoured to penetrate more deeply into the patient's unconscious mainly by interpreting his resistances.

Opinions were polarized. On the one hand was Ferenczi, an engaging, sincere man devoted to the clarification of interpersonal relationships and of his own feelings and reactions, who concluded that it is artificial for an analyst to try to keep his private life totally separate from his professional one; above all, he sought honesty in himself. On the other hand, there were those who preferred to establish rules that would be scientific and external— truths that would be reassuring in their objectivity. This trend was spearheaded by Wilhelm Reich.[2] In grappling with the problems posed by resistances, he had become aware of how important hostile feelings can be in psychoanalysis. For Reich, psychoanalysis was 'character analysis' and as such should bear on resistances as they are expressed not only in symptoms, but in the patient's behaviour, in his character. In Reich's view, *character analysis* and resistance analysis were one and the same thing. The analytic attitude that he recommended was to follow closely the *dynamics* of the analytic *process* and to raise resistances as they appeared. Like Ferenczi, Reich had always been keenly interested in problems of technique, to which he attributed great importance, proposing more open discussion of them at congresses (Lobner, 1978). According to Richard Sterba, 'Reich had a particular sensitivity for the recognition of latent resistances and their often hardly noticeable influence on the patient's conscious material. The form in which the patient presented his material, his manner and his peculiarity of speech, how he entered the office, how he shook hands with the analyst [in Vienna an established custom at the beginning and closing of each session]—all this Reich taught us to use as important information, particularly about latent resistances' (Sterba, 1982, p. 35).

Interest in character analysis placed new emphasis on the personality of the analysand but without focussing on the patient–analyst relationship. The later work of Anna Freud (1936) on defences is in the same tradition. It is a study of one person, the analysand, and not two, and aims at establishing a *one person* 'psychoanalytic psychology'. Significantly, throughout this period terminology continuously fluctuated between 'defence', an ego function, and 'resistance', a term referring to the analytic process.

As already pointed out, Reich viewed psychoanalysis as *character* analysis. Reich's 1928 article 'On Character Analysis' introduces the notion of 'coherency' of interpretation in the analysis of resistances, and remarks that unless the analyst proceeds by 'layers', the result will be a 'chaotic situation'. These observations clearly suggest that the analyst takes an active part in maintaining the analytic situation and in 'organizing' the material. They also imply that Reich was well aware of the analyst's contribution to the psychoanalytic process (cf. Reich, 1927, p. 146), but that he preferred to focus mainly on the patient's contributions. Reich discusses the analyst's interventions only from the viewpoint of interpretations as premature, inconsistent, trivial, and the like.

Such were the beginnings of a discussion between

analysts in favour of interpreting *resistance*—in other words, the unrecognized, unconscious components that oppose the unfolding of the therapeutic process—and those who aim, rather, at making *unconscious contents* conscious through interpretation. Some, like H. Kaiser (1934), a tragic and forgotten figure in psychoanalysis, believed that the analyst should direct his verbal interventions (interpretations) almost exclusively towards the *obstacles* that interfere with the therapeutic process and actively promote personal growth, respecting the order in which the analysand becomes aware of unconscious material. Others were more interested in naming the *contents* concealed behind resistances. These two opposing views may have fewer conflicting practical implications than the controversies surrounding them would lead us to suppose. Could it well be, for instance, that concentrating on the unconscious forces that act as *obstacles* to the treatment is precisely the best way to reveal the *contents* of the unconscious?

Reich held that the analyst should focus on the patient's aggressivity as a 'fight' against the psychoanalytic process and, as a last resort, against recall of *traumas*, and that he should systematically interpret it. Both Reich and Kaiser devoted much scientific effort to the study of resistance, and their endeavours finally succeeded in turning analytic attention to the *unconscious contrariness of analysands*.[3] Kaiser spoke of 'oppositional character',[3] whereas much later J. McDougall (1972) coined the word 'antianalysand'[3] to describe the same feature.

Strachey (1934) approached the problem from a different angle. His hypothesis was based on his conviction that resistance is always expressed in the transference. For him, extratransferential interventions were of only secondary importance. It is only when interpretations touch a 'point of urgency' of affects and resistances that they enable the patient to change: these are the '*mutative*' interpretations, a fundamental notion in the later development of psychoanalytic practice. As for latent negative transference and negative therapeutic reaction, Strachey considered them functions of the superego, which are taken care of by the introjection of the analyst. This concept was subsequently developed by Melanie Klein and her followers as the introjection of the image of the 'good' analyst.

Richard Sterba's well-known 1934 study of *introjection* in the analyst–analysand relationship, 'The Fate of the Ego in Analytic Therapy', distinguishes two parts of the ego in analysis: one engrossed in the experience of the session, the other in understanding that experience by identification with the analysing function of the analyst. Sterba's article ushered in a *new era*. As G. Bibring pointed out in 1932, resistance and transference, the two burning issues of the 1920s, would eventually be abandoned even at the Vienna seminars on psychoanalysis. First, however, there was an intermediate period initiated by Theodor Reik in 1933 when he deliberately undertook to temper what he considered to be an excess of intellectualization, drawing attention to the element of surprise in every analysis. He recommended that the analyst give free rein to his unconscious, without harbouring any preconceived notions—especially theoretical notions—about his patients. Essentially, Freud had said the same thing over twenty years earlier. 'The most successful cases are those in which one proceeds, as it were, without any purpose in view, allows oneself to be taken by surprise by any new turn in them, and always meets them with an open mind, free from any presuppositions' (Freud, 1912e, *12*:114). In this passage, he had already come close to a position in which the internal attitude of the analyst counts for more than 'technique'. The implication is that the analyst would *reach* the analysand's affect by *surprise*. This issue was later extensively developed by Bion (1967).

The 1920s and early 1930s were dominated by a search for rules supposed to provide a frame of reference for analysts—that of 'correct' Freudian psychoanalysis. The difficulties and deceptions, not to mention the hypocrisy towards the patient, that such a search entailed were inevitable, and *several techniques* created some perturbation in analytic circles. Glover's 1938 (1940) survey of psychoanalytic practice showed to what extent practice differed even among members of the same society, and that these differences, surprisingly, depended less on schools or affiliations than on people themselves. Was there then no such thing as a *standard* analytic technique? And why? It was through questions such as these that the interest in counter-transference and the personal equation of the analyst were developed. Several articles from this period directly reflect Ferenczi's influence. In one of them, published in 1936, on 'Psychological Traumatism and the Management of Transference', Sterba demonstrates the mutual interaction of psychoanalytic theory and technique. He notes: 'During the last few years of his life, Ferenczi, the most fertile, active and universal of the apostles of analysis, plunged anew into the technical problems of analysis. With rare vigor and youthful enthusiasm, he rediscovered pathways which had been abandoned and forgotten in the course of psychoanalytic history' (Sterba, 1936, p. 40). Sterba, however, recommended waiting in order to be in a better position to understand the implications of these last experiments of Ferenczi, feeling that the neocathartic technique revived the trauma theory.

As for Glover (1931), he was preoccupied in demonstrating the cathartic effect of inexact interpretations. For him the analyst's interventions, exact or not, could result in a reduction of tension. This, of course, presupposes knowing of what 'the exactitude' consists and how it is judged. The accent, in this case, is on the intensity of the analytic experience, over and above the *exactitude* of interpretation.

As if to put a final touch to the deliberations of that era so that psychoanalysts could move on to new fields of exploration, Fenichel summed up the oral tradition of the 1920s and early 1930s. He recorded the precepts of what was considered so-called classical technique. Every analyst in training has heard the following rules quoted, often without reference to the man who systematized them:

1. One should always start the interpretation at the surface ...

2. The patient determines the subject matter of the analytic hour ...
3. Interpretation of resistance precedes interpretation of content ...
4. We should avoid too deep or too superficial interpretations (Fenichel, 1941, pp. 44–45).

Although it was Fenichel who coined the phrase 'The subject matter, not the method, of psychoanalysis is irrational' (ibid., p. 13), Freud had already spoken in the same vein (Freud, 1914g, *12*:147; 1932c, *22*:220), and Fenichel's well-known saying aptly expresses Freud's longing to develop a rational technique, which would qualify psychoanalysis as a true science.

Fenichel also recorded remarks rightly or wrongly attributed to Freud: 'Freud once said that when the patient talks only of his present reality, the analyst must speak of his childhood; and the analyst must bring in present reality when the patient relates only childhood reminiscences. Theorizing about childhood relates only to a past that is not connected up with present reality, whereas "acting out" is present reality, the past character of which is not evident' (Fenichel, 1941, p. 20). 'Everything is permissible, if only one knows why' (ibid., p. 24).

But Fenichel was aware of the relative value of all these rules. Referring to a remark made by Freud in his 'Recommendations to Physicians Practicing Psychoanalysis' (Freud, 1912e), he adds: 'We must always be ready to let ourselves be led by the patient to something quite different from what we had expected' (Fenichel, 1941, p. 48). He also expresses his admiration for Theodor Reik's 1935 book *Surprise and the Psychoanalyst*, in which Reik had modified his standpoint on 'systematic techniques' 'in a gratifying way'. Fenichel points out that 'this splendid book contains the best scientific theory of the mode of action of intuition' (ibid., p. 109).

Fenichel underlined two points contained in the quotations introducing this chapter: how is it that we know so little about 'what *actually* takes place in a psychoanalytic treatment'; why are we still so ignorant about 'the analyst's part therein?' (ibid., p. 1).

What does the psychoanalyst do? What transpires within the framework of the treatment? These two questions had taken him far from his point of departure. In a post-humously published article (Fenichel, 1980 [1938]) he addresses the problem of training analysis, studies the psychology of the analyst, of the thought processes involved in analysing others, recalling the 'error which has its roots in the unconscious of the analyst'. In 1935[4] Fenichel clearly stated that the *instrument* of psychoanalytic technique is the analyst's unconscious.

Hindsight joined foresight in a very *lucid* article by Vilma Kovacs (Michael Balint's mother-in-law), who dates the beginning of the controversies between analysts at about the time of the 1913 Munich Congress. She writes:

> There was no longer even a trace of the sincerity and friendly co-operation which is to be expected amongst colleagues. Instead, there was strife, arising from unconscious passions and leading to regrettable divisions which, at the cost of grievous disappointment, brought home to Freud the momentous fact that analysts, no less than their patients, are subject to resistance to disagreeable truths. He found it no matter for surprise that a patient, even after attaining a certain degree of understanding, should, when confronted with new and painful discoveries, relinquish such insight as he had acquired: Freud's great disappointment sprang rather from the fact that he was forced to observe the same phenomenon in analysts (Kovacs, 1936, p. 348).

Trained by Ferenczi, Kovacs believed that these impassioned controversies derived from the *personality* of the analyst and his resistances.

The scene was thus set for the *fundamental* discussions of the analyst himself. The issue was to be *developed* at length in Alice and Michael Balint's 'On Transference and Counter-transference' (Balint & Balint, 1939a).

NOTES

1. In 1914, he was to write that the psychoanalyst 'employs the art of interpretation mainly for the purpose of recognizing the resistances ... and making the patient conscious of them' (Freud, 1914g, *12*:147).
2. As successor to Nunberg, Reich was director of the seminar on psychoanalytic technique in Vienna from 1924 to 1930. Over and above the recognition he had gained through his own research and writings, he enjoyed considerable official prestige as director of the seminar. His official position as well as his reputation undoubtedly account for his far-reaching influence on the analytic thinking and writing of that period.
3. These concepts bear great similarity to Freud's *negative therapeutic reaction,* a phenomenon he ascribed to 'a need for illness' through guilt (Freud, 1923b, *19*:49).
4. Implicitly referring to Freud (see Chapter 1).

CHAPTER FIVE

The analyst—the unknown— and his regressed patient: The work of Michael Balint

> I think I am one of the more historically minded people in these islands ...
>
> Balint to Jones, in a letter dated 25 October 1954

Balint, the analyst

At the celebrated 1932 Congress[1] at Wiesbaden, Michael Balint presented a paper entitled 'Character Analysis and New Beginning' (Balint, 1933e). In view of psychoanalytic developments over the preceding years, he proposed that analysts should henceforth reach beyond the analysis of symptoms and complexes to apprehend what *characterizes* the analysand. Balint's proposal implied that analysts should extend the scope of their awareness *to everything that makes* the patient a *unique individual*. Such a viewpoint changed the very perspectives of psychoanalysis, the classical aims of which—to make the unconscious conscious, to remove infantile amnesia, to overcome resistances—were to be reconsidered because neither the unconscious, nor infantile amnesia, nor resistances are ever done away with completely. 'Even after the end of an analysis', he was to specify later, 'at least so much remains unconscious in the mind as is necessary for dream formation, and enough resistance

71

unresolved to be able to disturb a dream-analysis considerably' (Balint, 1935c, in 1965a, p. 180).[2]

Others formulated the goals of psychoanalysis in somewhat different terms. Ferenczi and Rank had described the aim of analysis as 'the complete reproduction of the Oedipus relation in the analytic experience' (Ferenczi, 1924 [264]). Vilma Kovacs had said that it was 'the unwinding of the repetition factor' (Kovacs, 1931), while Wilhelm Reich was later to formulate it as 'attaining ... full genitality of orgastic potency' (Reich, 1933). For his part, Michael Balint set out to show how Ferenczi's 'new beginning' concept could be used to go beyond the repetition compulsion (Balint, 1935c).

In 1939, in a paper that was the last he and Alice were to write together, Balint approached the problem of transference. In his characteristically concrete style he wrote:

> The phenomenon of transference can best be demonstrated if its object is an inanimate, lifeless thing, e.g. the door which was banged because the cause of our anger was behind it. With a living being, the whole situation becomes infinitely more complex, because (a) the second person is also striving to get rid of his unvented emotions by transferring them on to the first, and (b) he will react to the emotions transferred on to him by the first person. The situation is hopelessly inextricable, unless one of the persons involved will voluntarily undertake the task of not transferring any of his feelings on to the other for a definite period, i.e. to behave as nearly as possible like an inanimate thing (Balint & Balint, 1939a, in Balint, 1965a, p. 201).

> Freud has emphasized the fact that analysis does not take place in an airtight compartment; the analyst has a name, is male or female, is of a particular age, has a home, etc.; in a very broad sense, we transfer these elements of our personality on to our patients (Balint, ibid., p. 202).

Unencumbered by the taboo that forbade even thinking about what went on in the analyst's mind, Balint went straight to the heart of matters, describing them in refreshingly simple, clear and often amusing terms.

A very typical detail of this kind is 'the problem of the cushion'. There are several solutions to this problem: (a) the cushion remains the same for every patient, but a piece of tissue paper is spread over it which is thrown away at the end of the hour; (b) the cushion remains, but every patient is given a special cover, distinguishable from the others by its shade or design, and for each hour the cushion is put into the appropriate cover; (c) each patient has his own cushion and must use only his; (d) there is only one cushion or only two or three of them for all the patients and it is left to them to use them as they like, etc. Moreover these possibilities have to be multiplied by at least three, because the situation differs according to whether the analyst, the patient or a servant manipulates the cushion.

A bagatelle, it may be thought, which it is almost ridiculous to treat at such length. And yet such trifles seem to have a certain importance in the formation of the transference situation. For instance, one patient, who for external reasons had had to change his analyst, dreamt of his first analyst as working in a highly modern, white-tiled W.C., well fitted with every hygienic refinement, and of the second as working in an old-fashioned, dirty, stinking place. It is not difficult to guess which solution of the 'problem of the cushion' was favoured by the first analyst and which by the second. The dream analysis showed clearly that the patient drew certain conclusions as regards his two analysts' different attitudes towards cleanliness from the way in which they treated the cushion problem. No one is likely to dispute that an analysis conducted in an atmosphere corresponding to the first part of the dream will take a different course from what it would in an atmosphere corresponding to the second part. For the present we are not concerned with the problem of whether or not one

Figure 4. Michael Balint working with doctors and psycho-analysts in August 1968 at the Château de Kernuz, Bretagne (photograph by Guy Lavallée, Paris).

condition is more favourable to the progress of an analysis than the other. We only wish to assert that there do exist differences in the analytical atmosphere which are brought about by the analyst himself. ...

The same is true of a whole number of such details. Another important point, for instance, is the way in which the end of the session is brought about. Some analysts get up from their chairs, thus giving the signal. Others simply announce it in stereotyped words; others again try to invent new formulas for each hour; some begin to move to and fro in their chairs and the patient has to infer from the sound that the time is over; others again use alarm clocks, or keep a clock in front of the patient so that he may himself see the time passing. Then there is the couch itself, which may be low, broad, comfortable, or quite the contrary; the chair of the analyst; the arrangement of the consulting room—shall it be furnished as a study or as a drawing-room? or shall it be left totally unfurnished apart from the couch and the chair?—the method of lighting the room, etc. (ibid., pp. 202–203).

By carefully examining such apparently extraneous details, Balint gradually approaches the central feature of the analyst's activity. 'Some analysts are parsimonious with their interpretations, and give one only when its correctness is practically certain; others are rather lavish, even at the risk of giving a number of incorrect ones' (ibid., pp. 203–204). He answers the question of what, when and how to interpret by saying that 'every analysis carried out by the same analyst is different from every other one; ... it is undeniable that there are several individually different ways of analysing, different analytical atmospheres' (ibid., p. 205). It will be recalled that when Balint wrote these lines, Glover had undertaken (in 1938) his research showing the different ways of working analytically even within the British Psychoanalytic Society (Glover, 1940). Balint was not content with a statistical record. He put *the analyst* at the centre of his own visual field. In so doing he continued Ferenczi's way of thinking, but with a level-headedness that Ferenczi did not always have. Balint was keen to understand the historical development of psychoanalytic technique. His careful observation of the most minute details enabled him to construct a convincing argument and to discern at the deepest levels the desire of the two protagonists—analyst and analysand—to rid themselves of their feelings by mutual projection. For this desire exists not only in the analysand but also in the analyst; beneath the well-ordered surface of the 'rules of interpretation', the analyst's personality plays a vital role, and is not each a 'mirror to the patient' *differently*?

The great merit of this article was to submit *the analyst* himself to analytical scrutiny. Balint could present his point of view on 'mutual analysis', rather more prudently than Ferenczi had done, having gained from Ferenczi's experience. The idea of multiple transferences of the two protagonists, and their multiple desires to rid themselves of unresolved problems, opened whole new perspectives. At the time, this idea seemed innovative, even though Freud himself spoke of the analyst's sensitivity as the tool of his work, 'an organ' enabling him to understand what was going on in the analysand (Freud, 1912e, *12*:115) and he had postulated the need for analysis of the analyst ('the training analysis') in order to specify elements that actually belong to the analyst and would 'contaminate' the analytic situation.

For Balint, his own 'emotional involvement', his counter-transference, would put the analyst in a position to 'reconstruct from the patient's association material and the symptoms of his transference neurosis, i.e. his repetition, the hypothetical traumatic situation' (Balint, 1968a, p. 115), while at the same time creating an atmosphere 'which will *not* then act as a stimulus provoking the eternal repetitions' (ibid.).

Balint re-examined the concept of regression from a historical point of view. Alluding to Freud's probable unease with the regressive phenomena (ibid., p. 121), he cites the article 'On the History of the Psycho-Analytic Movement', in which Freud is of the opinion that in order to resolve the effects of a recent trauma by analysis it was necessary to allow Dora to make 'a long detour leading back over her earliest childhood' (Freud 1914d, *14*:10). Balint observes how fallacious 'the neglect of regression in analytic technique' was (Balint, 1968a, p. 123). It is in the context of the management of regressed patients that he gave an accurate assessment of Ferenczi's experiments in a summary that has become a classic (ibid., pp. 112ff., 124ff., 150ff.).

In their 1939 article on transference and counter-transference, Alice and Michael Balint also emphasized the *analyst's* need to be able to work in a manner that *suits* him emotionally. Transference is not the exclusive privilege of the analysand; as we have seen, the analyst also has a tendency to rid himself of his feelings onto the analysand. In other words, transference has *multiple* functions in the relationship between analyst and analysand. The analysand provokes in the *analyst* emotions that he tends to externalize in his own way by sublimation, by thinking things through and so forth.

Citing examples from the subject of terminating analysis, they show how each analyst has his own way of proceeding, which suits him and which, moreover, he thinks is right: it is reminiscent of Freud's 'narcissism of minor differences' (Freud, 1930a, *21*:114). But it is not a matter of being right. Every analyst must be capable of *perceiving* what he does, what he creates, what he engenders. The contribution made by the Balints in Ferenczi's footsteps is the introduction of the analyst as a subject of observation. It is no longer sufficient to perceive exclusively the movements of the analysand, those of the analyst must be attended to as well, as Alice Balint had previously suggested (A. Balint, 1936, p. 55). The analyst has a right to seek some mental comfort in his work, to be truly himself in his analyst's chair; he must also fulfil his function of mirror vis-à-vis the analysand—a living mirror that *reflects in its own way* the analysand's 'truth' to him.

It is in this way that we come to realize that psychoanalysis is not only a technique; it is *much more* a relation between two people. At first, a technique is necessary for playing the piano, but the artist's interpretation is far more than technical execution. By the same token, the practice of psychoanalysis presupposes a certain amount of technique, but there is more to it than just that. Ferenczi's thoughts on technique lead to a higher order of analytic *practice*.

At the 1949 Zurich Congress, Balint made the following comment: 'The most important field of investigation for ... coming theory must be the *analyst's behaviour in the psycho-analytic situation*, or, as I prefer to phrase it, the analyst's contribution to the creating and maintaining of the psycho-analytic situation' (Balint, 1950, in 1965a, p. 218). And, with a keen sense for possible repercussions, he added, 'A very dangerous and awkward topic indeed ...' (ibid.).

For Balint, the majority of psychoanalytic studies are based on clinical observations and descriptions in which subjects are experiencing 'more or less complete *withdrawal from their objects*' (ibid., p. 214), as in obsessional and melancholic states. For other states, such as sexual disorders, he believed it was very important to examine the relationship to the object. Alluding to Rickman's suggestion, Balint stressed the need to view psychoanalysis as 'Two-Body-Psychology' (ibid., p. 222). Although he is close in this respect to Melanie Klein, he nevertheless charts his own course by turning his attention to the analyst's role in 'keeping the tension in the psycho-analytical situation at or near the optimal level' (ibid., p. 218). He points out that 'it is as true for the patient as for his analyst that no human being can in the long run tolerate any relation which brings only frustration, i.e. an ever-increasing tension between him and his object. Sooner or later the tension must be relieved. ...' He queries 'how much and what kind of satisfaction is needed by the patient on the one hand, and by the analyst on the other' (ibid.) and what role language and interpretation will play in the relief of tension (ibid., p. 219). The 'two-body' view, in which the *analyst* participates fully in the relation with his own economy and dynamics, with his own reactions and personality, seems to have been recognized as a basic stance for dealing with analytic problems.

In the article he co-authored with Tarachow, after these ideas seemed to have been acknowledged in psychoanalytic circles, Balint pointed out that psychoanalytic technique had *entered* an entirely *new phase* of development (Balint & Tarachow, 1952). Whereas previously attention had been focused on the analysand in the therapeutic process—in other words, on the transference—henceforth it would also scrutinize the analyst's participation in that process.

The search for primary love

Speaking of Michael Balint's stance on the controversy between London (Kleinian School), and Vienna (represented at the time by Waelder) over infantile mental development, Masud Khan remarks that he knows of 'no other analyst whose work so rigourously reflects, absorbs (and) critically evaluates the various trends of research at different phases of the psychoanalytic movement'. And he adds, 'What further characterizes Dr. Balint's writing, and it is a model we can well afford to emulate today, is that his responsiveness to the ideas of others is never unduly marred by rigid private convictions or militant factional loyalties' (Khan, 1969, p. 238). Thus, for example, Balint addresses the topic of the infantile mind: 'The obvious conclusion is that the present material is insufficient to allow of a decision in this issue ...' (Balint, 1962b, in 1965a, p. 79). 'Waelder [representing the then current Viennese school of thought on the matter] doubts whether the experiences of the very first developmental stages of the human mind can ever be recollected consciously' (ibid., p. 78). 'But it is at least equally certain that the experiences of this time are of paramount importance and essentially influence the whole later life of the individual ... but the question arises how can one get reliable data about these experiences?' (ibid., p. 79). He goes on to answer his own question in these terms: 'Our common starting point was to consider the formal elements of the analytical situation ... as phenomena of transference, hoping that in this way we might obtain valuable data ...' (ibid.).

Elsewhere he says that it was 'Sándor Ferenczi[3] who first called attention to the fact that the formal elements of the transference and the whole analytic situation derive from very early infant–parent relationships' (ibid., p. 145). He explores the 'primitive' stage of love as he felt he could reconstitute it from elements of the analytic situation.

Dealing with the problem of primary narcissism, he states: 'In my opinion it is the hypothesis of primary narcissism that mainly causes the confusion of tongues between Vienna and London' (ibid., p. 86), adding, ' ... Freud has emphasized that absolute narcissism in itself is impossible' (ibid., p. 87). Balint then proceeds to develop his own hypothesis on *primary love* (ibid.).

In Balint's view 'primary love'—the desire to 'be loved always, everywhere, in every way, my whole body, my whole being'—is the 'primary tendency' in transference (Balint, 1935b, in 1965a, p. 50). If the mother–child bond is unsatisfying from the start, the remainder of the individual's life will be spent seeking reparation for the missing primary love. For him, primary love is central to the degree that he felt narcissism is only a detour to obtain for oneself what others didn't give, and that aggression is no more than a reaction to this missing primary love (Balint, 1952c, in 1965a, p. 128).

Alice Balint, 'under the influence of Michael's ideas ... in which he emphasizes the active features of infantile behaviour', thought as early as 1939 that 'the term *passive* was inadequate for describing a relationship in which such markedly *active* tendencies as the instinct to cling play a paramount role'. For this reason, she preferred to use 'in place of "*passive object-love*" ... the terms "*archaic*" or "*primary object relationship*" *(object love)*' (A. Balint, 1939, p. 108). Her formulations foreshadowed the recent observations of specialists in early infant development.

During that same period Balint correlated his views on the intra-analytic relationship with contemporary hypotheses about the archaic object-relationship. In the 1950s and early 1960s he was engaged in some of his most productive thinking, greatly clarifying many aspects of regression. He endeavoured to put regression in relation to the notion of mental balance and health. 'Is health the result of a lucky chance, a rare or even an improbable event, the reason being that its conditions are so stringent and so numerous that the chances are very heavily weighted against it?'

(Balint, 1950b, in 1965a, p. 226). He observed that those 'who think that mature genitality is not simply a chance sum-total of a motley mixture of component sexual instincts but a function *per se*, also think that health is a "natural" equilibrium and the termination of a psycho-analytic cure is a "natural" process' (ibid.). In an article published in honour of Melanie Klein's seventieth birthday, he affirmed that this process is closely related to the problem of love. 'I consider ... *primitive, or archaic, object-love* ... to be the *fons et origo* of human libido development. The original and everlasting aim of all object-relations is the primitive wish: *I must be loved* without any obligation on me and without any expectation of return from me' (Balint, 1952b, in 1965a, p. 233). In the same article he made an important observation: ' ... as long as we have hardly any well-founded knowledge of the dynamisms governing the relation of the various technical approaches to their respective theoretical findings, we have no choice but to accept most analytic techniques as peers'. This was Balint's way of responding to the challenge that had resulted from Glover's 1940 survey of analytic practice. But Balint was aware of the fact that such an affirmation was true only within certain limits and he added 'except a few obviously faulty ones! The reason why I abstain from including this rider is that for the present I cannot see any criteria which would enable us to decide objectively what is an "obviously faulty" technique and what is not, although, like every other analyst, subjectively I am convinced that doubtless there are some "obviously faulty" techniques' (ibid., p. 246).

In the analytic process, equilibrium and the realization of potential proceeds from a *new beginning,* which is 'the capacity for an unsuspicious, trusting, self-abandoned and relaxed object-relation' (ibid., p. 241). It is arrived at after the *paranoid* attitude has been relinquished and the necessary *mourning* effected, which then enables expression of 'the sequence: paranoid attitude—depression—primary object-love' (ibid., p. 242). In other words: '(a) the relinquishing of the paranoid attitude, the realization that the paranoid anxieties were unfounded or at least grossly exaggerated; (b) the acceptance, without undue anxiety, of a certain amount of depression as an inevitable condition of life, and the confidence that it is possible—but not certain—to emerge from this kind of depression a better man' (ibid., pp. 241–242). Such a development by means of regression is the necessary precursor of every new beginning. In its historical context, the emergence of this concept is interesting in so far as Balint felt indebted to Daniel Lagache and Melanie Klein who both contributed to a better understanding of the 'new beginning' (letter, 20 May 1951, to Daniel Lagache).

Writing to Martin Grotjahn, he wondered: 'I cannot see why any analyst should be afraid of fostering "a dependent, infantile, regressive transference relationship". I must say that in my analyses this stage is almost always reached whether by candidates or patients; moreover, my whole idea of a new beginning, which is of paramount importance, I think, for a proper termination of analysis, presupposes such a situation as a transitory period' (letter to Grotjahn, 10 February 1954, Balint Archives of Geneva [Switzerland]).

'Provided the analyst is able to fulfil most of the requirements ... and grants his patient a sufficiently long, in some cases very long, period of violent aggressiveness followed by mourning and regret about the original fault or failure and all the losses caused by it ... a new relationship may develop which will enable the patient to experience a kind of regret or mourning' (Balint, 1968a, p. 183). 'The period of mourning must be allowed to run its course which, in some patients, may be exasperatingly long. Although this process cannot be hurried, it is most important that it should be witnessed; ... apparently it is impossible to go through this mourning by oneself; it can be done only in the framework of a two-person relationship, such as the analytic situation' (ibid., p. 184). 'This mourning is connected with the giving up of a narcissistic picture of oneself ... the process of mourning discussed here is about giving up for good the hope of attaining the faultless ideal of oneself' (ibid., footnote, p. 183). Balint discusses this process in connection with patients who are 'difficult to place ... under any diagnostic heading. Their chief complaint is that they cannot find their place in life. ... They take no pleasure in anything' (Balint, 1933e, in 1965a, p. 151). Although he is referring—like Ferenczi, the 'specialist of hopeless cases'—only to analytic patients who have not attained the oedipal level, one might wonder whether this dimension of failure with respect to a narcissistic megalomaniac ideal does not exist in all human beings. It would seem, after all, necessary to presume that everybody has a weak or faulty zone, an area of basic traumas, with more or less significant consequences.

The *study* of regression in analysis or, as Balint put it, the study of 'The Regressed Patient and His Analyst' (Balint, 1960c), is guided by a general principle that is applicable to all human beings: The human foetus is extremely *dependent* on its environment, infinitely more so than the baby or the adult. As a result, it is essential for its well-being and development that its environment should provide all that it needs. Any significant lack is life-threatening.

Balint considers that this biological situation is a model for the distribution of its libido in the course of the foetal life and deduces that its cathexis of the environment must be very intense. This environment, however, remains undifferentiated: it does not yet contain objects and practically no structures. It is a 'harmonious interpenetrating mix-up', the model for which is a fish in the sea. This harks back to the image sketched by Balint's teacher Ferenczi in 'Thalassa'. It would be idle to ask whether the water in the fish's gills is part of the sea or of the fish. The foetus, the amniotic fluid, the placenta, exist as interpenetrating elements. Our relation to the air that surrounds us is similar: we cannot do without it; at times it is inside us, in our lungs, at times outside; it is simply there; it gives us life without our noticing its existence. We do not consider it as an object (in its derivation from the Latin *ob-jectus,* meaning something that is 'thrown against us'). There is a latent cathexis which becomes apparent only when air is lacking.

Birth can be viewed as a trauma (reminiscent of the ideas of Ferenczi's erstwhile friend Otto Rank) that brings about the first separation between the individual and his environment. Contrary to friendly substances, objects take on definite, sharply defined shapes that must be recognized and respected. An object presents a painful contrast to the previous peaceful harmony. Part of the libido will withdraw into the ego: this is secondary narcissism. But 'the discovery that there are independent solid and separate objects destroys the world (of the harmonious mix-up). Henceforth, ... the existence of objects must be recognized, with their attributes of resistance, aggressivity and ambivalence'. There are two basic ways of reacting to this traumatizing discovery: 'The one consists in creating an ocnophilic[4] world based on the fantasy that solid objects are benevolent and trustworthy, that they will always be there when needed and that they will never object to anything. The other reaction is to create a philobatic[4] world' and develop a certain measure of independence with respect to objects (Balint, 1959a, p. 67 passim).

In the ocnophilic reaction, the subject holds fast to the object, overestimates it and becomes dependent on it. In philobatism, the subject makes himself independent of the object and tries to stress his own (ego) aptitudes in the 'objectless expanses' (Balint, 1968a, p. 72). Balint's description sheds new light on Melanie Klein's concept of the images of the 'good' and 'bad' mother, by affirming that children cannot understand why parents sometimes act one way, sometimes another. The *trauma* was also to have been treated in *incomprehensible* fashion: this is Balint's version of Ferenczi's 'confusion of tongues'.[5] In Balint's opinion, splitting is secondary. 'In the eyes of the child his parents are capricious beings who, quite unaccountably, are sometimes bad to him and sometimes good. And the more neurotic the behaviour of the parents, the harder is the task of adjustment for the child, who, in the end, has no choice but to treat his mother, for instance, as two fundamentally different beings. Sometimes the "fairy" is there, and sometimes the "witch"' (Balint, 1935c, in 1952a, p. 186).

Zones of maturation and of regression

Balint arrives at the conclusion that distinct zones can be determined according to the degree of psychological—and, in particular, affective—maturity. One of these zones is the Oedipus complex, characterized by the presence of conflict and ambivalence and by frustrations that can be verbally communicated. Freud established a framework within which patients are able to communicate their experiences in the form of problems. Psychoanalysis enables them to understand themselves better (what is called 'insight'). Surprisingly, the definition of the oedipal zone is a criterion of counter-transference. 'Will this analysis be rewarding or unrewarding [for the analyst]? With some malice one could even say that one of the questions asked is whether the patient is likely to bring satisfaction to his analyst' (Balint, 1968a, p. 101).

While the oedipal level involves three people, in the zone of the basic fault there are only two: the *fault* is the absence of the structuring third person. This relation between two people 'is not that obtaining between two adults; it is more primitive ... the force originating from the basic fault has *not* the form of a conflict' (ibid., pp. 28–29). In passing, Balint makes several extremely important theoretical observations—e.g., 'Usually it is assumed that the phenomena observed clinically in the psychoanalytic situation can be taken as a representative sample of the whole of human development ... I think it is absolutely false', he said with unaccustomed emphasis. 'First, not everything that happens in human development is repeated in the psychoanalytic situation; and second, what is repeated is profoundly distorted by the conditions prevailing there' (ibid.).

Balint was a linguist and very sensitive to language and translation problems, which crop up on several different levels in psychoanalysis. He deplored the fact that the science of semantics was still in its initial phases and thus unable to assist in exploring the 'clusters of associations surrounding each word' (ibid., p. 95). His remarks on words for feelings, affects, inner experiences, foreshadow many contemporary discussions. In particular, he was well aware that the different usages of a word in different languages pose problems for the translation of psychoanalytic literature. This applies first to Freud's work, and Balint says that 'Freud could never have developed his theory of *Besetzung* in English as there was no word available to express what he meant. As is well known, "*cathexis*" was made to measure to fill a gap, but it is improbable that it will ever be a living word. The same is true, still more, about *Lust* and *Unlust*. On the other hand, our modern theory of "*depression*" could develop only in English, in which this word covers a vague and widely extended field—in the same way as *Besetzung* or *Abwehr* does in German. The German *deprimiert* with its narrow and almost solid cluster of associations would have discouraged any such use right from the start' (ibid.). 'The German *Lust* and *Unlust* are simply untranslatable; the English "pleasure" means something utterly different, while "unpleasure" is a clumsy neologism' (ibid., p. 94).

Balint touches on the problems of verbal expression in regressive states. At the level of the basic fault, we translate the patient's primitive behaviour into conventional adult language. The Kleinians invented a very characteristic '"mad" language' that their patients learn to speak (ibid., p. 105). 'Their interpretations create the impression of originating from a confident, knowledgeable, and perhaps even overwhelming analyst', which 'might be one of the reasons why, on the one hand, so much aggressiveness, envy, and hatred emerges in their patients' association-material and, on the other hand, why they seem to be concerned so much with introjection and idealization' (ibid., p. 107). He wonders how the analysand organizes his communications by relying on words learned from his analyst, then, by analogy, he wonders how physicians, with their words, organize the illness of their patients. Balint considers that, for a true understanding of psychoanalytic practice, the analyst's behaviour, his respect for the patient as a person, must be taken into account as well as his responsibility in setting up the analytic framework. 'The analyst must accept the regression ... create an environment, a climate, in which he and his patient can tolerate the regression in a mutual experience' (ibid., p. 177) and 'provide ... sufficient time free from extrinsic temptations, stimuli, and demands, including those originating from himself (the analyst); the aim is that the patient should be able to find himself, to accept himself, and to get on with himself ..., he must be allowed to discover *his* way to the world of objects—and not be shown the "right" way' (ibid., pp. 179–180). 'Apart from being a "need-recognizing" and perhaps even a "need-satisfying" object, the analyst must be also a "need-understanding" object who, in addition, must be able to communicate his understanding to his patient' (ibid., p. 181). For Balint, the capacity to regress is an aptitude of patients; they cannot achieve it without a particular atmosphere of mutual confidence, which depends on the tact and skill of the analyst, an analyst who must be a discreet ordinary person, who does not offer himself as an omniscient and omnipotent object for clinging to, but who makes it possible to create a relationship in which the patient can find himself. The study of regressive states leads Balint to distinguish between two forms. 'In the one form the regression is aimed at gratification of instinctual cravings; what the patient seeks is an external event, an action by his object. In the other form what the patient expects is not so much an external action, but a tacit consent to use the external world in a way that would allow him to get on with his internal problems'. This is what one of Balint's patients called 'being able to reach himself'. Balint suggested calling the first type 'regression aimed at gratification' and the second 'regression aimed at recognition' (ibid., p. 144). For Balint, the second or 'benign' type of regression—trusting, confident, relaxed—is a necessary condition for a new beginning. When confronted with regression aimed at recognition '. . . the analyst must not resist, must consent, must not give rise to too much friction, must accept and carry the patient for a while, must prove more or less indestructible, must not insist on maintaining harsh boundaries ... all this means consent, participation, and involvement, but *not* necessarily action: ... [it signifies] understanding and tolerance' (ibid., p. 145). By differentiating between this 'benign' and a 'malignant' type of regression, the second being characterized by despair and passion, Balint approached in many respects the distinction suggested by Ernst Kris between 'the ego overwhelmed by regression' and 'regression in the service of the ego' (ibid., p. 153).

In 1968, just two years before his death, Balint once more questioned established practice. He noted that 'nowadays analysts are enjoined to interpret everything that happens in the analytic situation ... in terms of transference, i.e. of object relationship' (ibid., p. 175). He tried to clarify the unexpected consequences of technique as it was practiced in the latter half of the 1960s. 'This otherwise sensible and efficient technique means that we offer ourselves to our patients incessantly as objects to cling to, and interpret anything contrary to clinging as resistance, aggressiveness, narcissism, touchiness, paranoid anxiety, castration fear, and so on' (ibid.). A better understanding of transference–counter-transference phenomena should make it possible to measure the effect that the manner and style of interpreting can have on the analysand and on the relations between the two protagonists. According to his manner, the analyst can be experienced as omnipotent or omniscient, or as a separate object, with a sharply defined shape.

The number 'three' characterizes the zone of the Oedipus complex, while 'two' belongs to the zone of the basic fault. A third zone 'is characterized by the fact that in it there is no external object present. The subject is on his own and his main concern is to produce something out of himself' (ibid., p. 24). This zone is that of artistic, mathematical, philosophical creation, of the acquisition of insight, of the capacity to understand others 'and last, but not least, two highly important phenomena: the early phases of becoming ... "ill" and spontaneous recovery from an "illness"' (ibid.). This is similar to Bion's alpha and beta elements, and alpha function. Naturally, of course, it also applies to the silent patient, who generally 'runs away from' conflict, but who also 'runs toward something, i.e. a state in which he feels relatively safe ... a kind of "creation", ... a product of his creativity' (ibid., p. 26). In this process, there is neither object-relation nor transference, 'there is no outside object involved ... that is why our knowledge of these processes is so scanty and uncertain' (ibid., p. 29). This 'area of creation' is connected with the dimension of need, of disillusionment, of consecutive introjection and of the enrichment of the ego by philobatism. It is non-traumatic need. By this detour, we rediscover frustration, even the frustration caused by the analyst in the analytic situation, frustration that the 'discreet and unobtrusive' analyst considers as positive for the analysand. Here we find a clue to understanding the subject in his interactions with the world in which he lives—in its richness and multiplicity—with his limits and his potentialities.

Transmission in psychoanalysis

In the context of analytic work as it was conceived by Ferenczi and Balint, especially regarding the involvement of the person of the analyst, problems of training were of the greatest importance. Balint was astonished at the paucity of publications on the subject. 'Jones [pointed out] that it was very likely owing to insufficient interest', and Balint then goes on to rectify this statement, 'I would call it a severe inhibition' (Balint, 1948b, in 1965a, p. 255). 'This kind of inhibited thinking is the first suspicious symptom about

training. The second symptom ... is the tendency of our
training system to be dogmatic' (ibid., p. 256). He compares
it to 'initiation rites' that consist of 'forcing the candidate to
identify himself with his initiator, to introject the initiator
and his ideals, and to build up from these identifications a
strong superego which will influence him all his life ...
[whereas] what we consciously intend to achieve with our
candidates is that they should develop a strong critical ego,
capable of bearing considerable strains, free from ... any
automatic transference or thinking patterns' (ibid., p. 261).
Balint recapitulates the history of training. At first, there
was no systematized, organized *training*. 'There was no
attempt at a superego intropression,[6] nor any demand for a
forced identification. This led to several secessions' (ibid.,
pp. 267–268). Later, after the 1918 Budapest Congress,
'psycho-analysis created an efficient system of training and
a strong organization to enforce its standards. ... [This]
meant the establishment of a strong paternal authority "to
instruct and to admonish" and a firm pressure on the
candidate to make him accept his analyst's teachings, to
make him identify himself with them. By creating unneces-
sary tensions between the generations, this period led to
recurring strifes and resulted in the complete breakdown of
any central authority'. In the third period there were
'several claimants to loyalties in sharp competition one with
another ... thus there is little cooperation, but mainly
competition, between the groups' (ibid., p. 268).

Balint observes that with the coming of the third
generation of training analysts 'the various "schools"
within the analytical movement started' (Balint, 1954c, in
1965a, p. 278). He says that 'until then, any real controversy led to a secession. The reason for the more or less
friendly co-existence of rival "schools" within the analytical
movement since the twenties is partly that the differences
are less fundamental, but also that psycho-analysis has
become strong enough to tolerate—though suffering under
the strain—the struggle of conflicting ideas' (ibid., footnote). 'Not mentioning the impact of controversial ideas

upon training would make the whole present discussion hypocritical and false' (ibid., p. 279). He attempts to show the importance that this rivalry between schools may have for training analysts, particularly when they undertake re-analyses. 'The second analyst was not able to avoid becoming involved in the resentful atmosphere. To prevent the development of such hypercritical, almost hostile; sentiments ... new techniques had to be developed' (ibid.). In dealing with the problems involved in training analyses, Balint simultaneously traces the history of certain controversies. He recalls that different concepts relative to training analyses succeeded one another: the concept of demonstrating the existence of the unconscious; then the one Ferenczi put forward in 1928, which holds that a training analysis must be more thorough than a therapeutic analysis, 'a fully completed analysis' (Ferenczi, 1928 [282], *FIN.*, p. 84), which leads to a concept of training analyses that Balint calls 'supertherapy'. He adds that the problems connected with such analyses are never publicly discussed.

Balint points out that this situation has far-reaching consequences, particularly with respect to 'premature' interpretation of the hostility of the 'negative transference'—and this even though Freud (1937c) had strongly advised against it. 'As I believe this is the only instance when Freud uttered such a grave warning and psychoanalysis, disregarding the master's advice, developed exactly in the contra-indicated direction, the whole problem merits close examination' (Balint, 1954c, in 1965a, p. 281). He thinks that 'too early and too consistent interpretation of slight signs of hatred' has as a consequence that 'real hatred and hostility are only talked about, never felt, and are eventually repressed by the taboo of idealization ... the analyst must be "swallowed whole", as a whole, ever repaired and idealized object' (ibid., p. 282). In summary, he sees in this the origin of the different schools of 'supertherapy' resulting in 'a confusion of tongues'. He hopes that a new period will be devoted to reflection, to research, with respect to all these problems.

In his thinking Balint not only works against all dogmatism and taboos, but proposes a constant analytic scrutiny of situations between analysts that have an effect on analyses.

A study of doctors

Ferenczi had shown interest in the psychological aspect of medical practice even before meeting Freud and had published several articles on the subject (Lorin, 1983). One of his last, published in 1933, is entitled 'Freud's Influence on Medicine' (Ferenczi, 1933 [293], *FIN.*, p. 143ff.) and is a general survey of Freud's contributions to medicine. In his posthumous articles, too, we discover notes entitled 'Brief Presentation of Psychoanalysis for General Practitioners'[7] (Ferenczi, 1936 [297]). He constantly sought ways 'to give a more favourable prognosis for certain organic conditions by systematic psychoanalytic observation' (translated from the French: Ferenczi, 1982, p. 193). Moreover, he observes that 'the personality of the physician often has a greater effect on the patient than the medicine prescribed' (ibid.). This observation is the point of departure for Michael Balint's ideas on medical education.

Ferenczi had devoted considerable thought to the psychology of physicians and its repercussions on patients. 'Psycho-analysis demands of the physician untiring sensitivity to all of the patient's ideational associations, his emotions, and his unconscious processes. For this it is necessary that the physician himself have a flexible, plastic mind. He can attain this only by being analysed himself. How the future medical student will acquire this profound self-knowledge is a difficult question to answer' (Ferenczi, 1933 [293], *FIN.*, p. 153).

By way of reply, Balint set up 'training and research groups' for general practitioners, on the lines of the Hungarian psychoanalytic training system. Before the development of the Berlin Institute's so-called 'tripartite' training system, which calls for personal analysis, courses on theory, and supervision, the Budapest school made no such clear-cut distinction between these three aspects of training. Hungarian candidates associated freely in their own analyses around the cases they were treating. Inspired by this experience, Balint thought that it should be possible to create a training for general practitioners that would bring about 'a limited though considerable change in the doctor's personality' (Balint, 1961c, p. 7), allowing a better understanding of the doctor–patient relationship. Balint's premise was that any emotion felt by the physician in treating a patient should be considered a symptom of the illness. Balint introduced into medical practice methods for using the unconscious of doctor and patient to understand the true meaning of the communication—of the demand and the response.

The main features of these studies (aside from several precursory articles, e.g. Balint, 1926a and 1926d) were introduced in a 1955 article, 'The Doctor, His Patient and the Illness' (Balint, 1955b); this article was subsequently expanded and published under the same title in book form. The 1955 article focuses on the physician, on his 'apostolic function', on his role in organizing the illness by his interventions, by what he says and when and how he says it.

The time has not yet come to make a definitive evaluation of 'Balint Groups', as they are called in Europe, but it would seem that Balint's dream of promoting the psychological dimension of medical education has only partially come true. It should be pointed out that Freud's dream hardly fared better: it is questionable whether analysts have really made the most of Freud's ideas, particularly with respect to the therapeutic value of analysis. Even though Balint's training has enabled some practitioners to reach a better understanding of their own motives and of the dynamics involved in the doctor–patient relationship, it must be realized that there is a very real risk of 'deviation' from the original aims of the method, thereby transforming the Balint group into a self-experience, social-reform or 'short-term psychodynamic' group. While psychoanalysis has left an indelible mark on twentieth-century thought, mores and culture, the effects of the Balint movement have remained more circumscribed, though enriching within their own field.

Whereas psychoanalysis creates the analytic situation, Balint created a forum, a *space*, where the analyst and the doctor can meet. He believed that groups moderated by a non-analyst would not accomplish the same purposes. Balint was a scientific thinker. It was his ability to avoid all hint of dogmatism that enabled him to make psychoanalytic thinking a part of medical and scientific tradition.

In the wake of the controversy surrounding Ferenczi

As we have seen, the controversy between Freud and Ferenczi revolves around two issues. The first of these is the scope of transference. Ferenczi viewed *all* clinical phenomena—every experience in the analytic situation—as being potentially linked to the transference and therefore as a repetition of the past. The second issue relates to the fact that Ferenczi came to understand, in 1909, that in the transference neurotics help themselves 'by taking into the ego as large as possible a part of the outer world' (Ferenczi, 1909 [67], *FIR.*, p. 47). This *tremendous yearning*, this addiction and the 'pathological widening ... of [the] ego' (ibid., p. 48) are directly related to the impact of parental deficiencies—traumas. The controversy had reached this stage when Ferenczi died.

Ferenczi's conflict with Freud was initially a matter of personal differences, but it gradually spread to the Committee and affected an ever-widening circle of members highly influential in the psychoanalytic movement of the times. Balint was undoubtedly more diplomatic than his mentor Ferenczi; one of the reasons for this may have been the fact that he was not personally involved in such a conflict himself. Although Ferenczi clearly perceived what he called 'the pathology of societies'—in other words institutional conflicts—he was also rather naive and idealistic. He therefore hoped that things would be different between psychoanalysts. But little by little personal conflicts developed (such as the rivalry between Abraham and Ferenczi), in which Freud intervened with questionable judgement by writing, 'Though my personal intimacy with Rank and Ferenczi has increased because of geographical reasons, you ought to have complete confidence that you stand no lower than they in my friendship and esteem', and by admonishing Abraham not to overestimate the effects of conflicting views on the movement as a whole: '. . . we could remain under the same roof with the greatest of equanimity' (Freud's letter to Abraham, 4 March 1924, in Freud, 1965a, p. 353).

Then tensions arose between the Berlin Institute, the first formal school for psychoanalytic training, on the one hand, and Vienna and Budapest on the other. Freud himself was not convinced that the Berlin model of systematic teaching was the ideal solution (Sterba, 1982). Training was less structured in Budapest, perhaps as a reflection of the less systematic, more individually inclined Budapest character. Ferenczi and, later, Balint—even after he had settled in London—did their best not to separate personal analysis and early supervision. It was the rule in Budapest that a candidate's own analyst supervised the candidate's first case—one example, but a significant one, of the differences in training. During the 1920s, every city worked out its own solution: London, under the influence of Jones and later, increasingly, of Melanie Klein; Berlin, very systematic; and Budapest on an apparently more flexible model (with many more patients in analysis than elsewhere) and with an informal training and out-patient consultations, which later became the Budapest Institute and Policlinic.

When Ferenczi died in 1933, Balint was very involved in the scene. His 'tact' enabled him to participate in general developments, in the exchange of ideas, while at the same time realizing that he belonged to the fringe group.[8]

One incident that helped bring these conflicts out into the

open was Balint's rebuttal of Jones' views over the circumstances surrounding Ferenczi's illness and death. Jones was already ill at that time, and on that account certain analysts did not want to take issue with him. Fromm wrote an article in which he evaluated Balint's letter to the editor of the *International Journal of Psycho-Analysis,* and Jones' response to it. Fromm notes: 'Balint's letter hardly needs any comment. Here is an honest and intelligent man, a pupil and close friend of Ferenczi. He feels obliged to present the facts as he observed them and to correct Jones' statement about his teacher's alleged mental illness ("paranoid schizophrenia"). He points out that until the day of his death Ferenczi, who suffered from pernicious anaemia, was always mentally clear. This is an unequivocal statement which implies that Jones' statement was untrue' (Fromm, 1970; footnote, p. 20). And, further on: 'If such a tortuous and submissive letter had been written by a lesser person than Balint, or if it had been written in a dictatorial system in order to avoid severe consequences for freedom or life, it would be understandable. But considering the fact that it was written by a well-known analyst living in England, it only shows the intensity of the pressure which forbids any but the mildest criticism of one of the leaders of the Organization' (ibid., p. 21, continuation of footnote from p. 20).

Probably Balint, like Ferenczi, was convinced that he was working in direct line with Freud's fundamental discoveries. At the same time, both men were aware of the difficulty in suggesting, and rendering acceptable, alternatives to prevalent psychoanalytic theory. Ferenczi probably felt more rejected and had greater fear of not being loved. Balint defended his position with more diplomacy, with the deference towards elders and authority figures characteristic of his generation in Central Europe. He had greater resources than Ferenczi—especially the unshakeable conviction that he was right and was entitled to defend his views.

Balint was unswerving in his loyalty to Ferenczi. He was convinced that Ferenczi had been the victim of flagrant injustice. He never concealed his fondness for his teacher. In 1961 he humorously remarked when referring to Ferenczi in an address to colleagues, 'because of my still unresolved transference' (Balint, 1962b, in 1965a, p. 145) and drove the point home a little later on with, 'a further phenomenon of my unresolved transference' (ibid., p. 147). But. stronger still than his 'central European' self-irony was his conviction that Ferenczi's ideas were profound observations that would be of great benefit to the analytic community. His work has contributed to that.

Balint's scientific position

The scientific and epistemological framework of meta-psychology has changed constantly during the course of psychoanalysis. For this reason it is necessary to establish the ties each thinker maintained with the metapsychological tradition. Balint's approach was to *rethink* meta-psychology within a new cultural context, in the light of his own experiences and those of Ferenczi. He wanted to contribute to the development of what he always considered a science and not to abandon it to espouse pure empiricism or impoverished commentary. Balint wanted to work in the *Freudian tradition* and within Freud's conceptual framework; this is what sets him apart from Fairbairn, whose ambition was to *create*, in the footsteps of Melanie Klein, a new conceptual framework for psychoanalysis. Balint's work is basically that of a *psychoanalytic thinker*. His firm loyalty to Freud is coupled with an independence of thought whose origins may be traced back to Ferenczi's example. Ferenczi's work was brought to fulfilment by Balint, who was not so much his pupil as his successor. Balint was passionately interested in psychoanalytic practice and unfearing in the questions he raised, such as its impact on psychoanalysts themselves (in terms of the counter-transference). His works, however, extend beyond the confines of psychoanalysis, one example being his activity in discussion groups with doctors. He sought to determine how psychoanalytic thought could be applied to other fields, such as the treatment of children or of somatic patients. In the eyes of those for whom Freud's profound insights should not be limited to an elite group, but rather permeate the cultural activity and human relations of our times, Balint's work was the act of a pioneer.

Balint was always interested in the foundations of psychoanalytic theory, as well as in striking a balance between the contributions of biology and the social sciences to psychoanalysis. Correspondence between Balint and Fenichel recently published by Russel Jacoby shows Balint leaning in the direction of what has been called 'the Freudian left' (Jacoby, 1983). Balint's letters express appreciation to Reich, Fenichel and others for having underlined the importance of social factors in the evolution of mankind. He had already shown keen interest in this topic, which he discussed at length with his first wife, Alice Balint, as well as with his friend and colleague Géza Róheim.

Trained in the natural sciences and 'coming from medicine and strongly biased by my predilection for the exact sciences' (Balint, 1952a, in 1965a, p. vii), Balint was acutely alert to methodological problems. Moreover, he had a particular feel for the historical development of psychoanalytic concepts. He strove to understand the *why* of controversies and to contribute to a better comprehension of them by endeavouring to understand theoretical divergencies in historical terms 'to trace back the differences in the theoretical constructions to the different points of view, the different expectations, and the different terms used' (Balint, 1968a, p. 75).[9]

Balint, the psychoanalytic investigator

Balint shares one feature common to all great psychoanalytic investigators: his ability to *transcend taboos*. The great psychoanalytic discoveries were made by *overcoming* resistances, even the occasional collective ones. Balint's inborn curiosity enabled him to push back the frontiers of knowledge, as is done in any scientific discovery or intellectual adventure.

Although Balint was prudent in his manner of expression, he challenged several concepts, always after rigorous examination. One example of this was his challenge of the concept of narcissism, which paved the way for Kohut on the one hand and for Lacan's 'mirror stage' on the other. He did not hesitate to call Abraham's classification of instincts 'rigid' and to plead for more flexible intellectual systems in conceptualizing the pregenital organization of the libido (Balint, 1935b, in 1965a, p. 38). At one fell swoop, he demolished widespread equations such as 'active = masculine' and 'passive = feminine' (Balint, 1936a, in 1965a, p. 63). He challenged the reification of psychoanalytic concepts, particularly in his book on regression (Balint, 1959a). He dealt with the problem of language in psychoanalysis (ibid.). He detected implicit problems in reconstruction and interpretation (Balint, 1954c). He opened up new vistas in the understanding of training (Balint, 1948b).

In investigating certain aspects of 'human nature' Balint gave priority to *experience* over theoretical abstractions. His study of human sexuality, for instance, is chiefly concerned with real life and Eros as experience. He contributed to a revision of the notion of perversion, a ubiquitous *experience* of sexual fantasies, the acting out of profound desire and fear. He also showed how speaking of 'partial' drives could lead to value judgements and pointed out how exceptional are states of total integration. His questioning of the concept of 'genital love' (Balint, 1948a), a notion tainted with elements of the superego, is another aspect of his lucid criticism. His pioneering role in all these fields is insufficiently acknowledged, perhaps due to his quiet, unostentatious presence, his aversion to creating a school, or, as we have seen, to his awareness of his own marginal position.

In one of his articles, Balint (1956b) painstakingly analysed Fairbairn's thesis that the libido is primarily 'object-seeking' rather than 'pleasure-seeking'. Balint shows that such a formulation arose only because of the artificial nature of the word 'libido', a word far from the original German *Lust*. The etymological investigation whereby he examines the nuances and meanings of different terms is characteristic of his work. He seems to formulate extremely important issues en passant, such as his remark that the analytic situation is not the same as the infantile situation: the mother is more gratifying, the analyst more frustrating, so that the childhood situation cannot be automatically compared to the analytic situation, or his observation that in describing new psychological phenomena it is imperative to record the emotional climate and the situational pressures under which they are observed. He emphasized that 'There is no such thing as an infant by himself' (Balint, 1956b, in 1956a, p. 287); and he also described the pregenital gratifications of the analytic situation, 'offering the patient complete freedom of speech; or a feeling of pleasant, fairly warm, friendly security by the analyst's providing a comfortable couch and a normally heated room, etc., and, above all: by creating the most gratifying, in the true sense unique, feeling in the patient that his analyst will be safely there, listening in a friendly and sympathetic way to the revelations of the patient's whole personality' (ibid., p. 286).[10]

In such a sensitive field, which requires above all human warmth and precludes brilliant demonstration, his original and profound thoughts also gave rise to negative reactions and hard feelings. Despite all this, the current consensus is that 'Balint [is] incontestably a forerunner ... of a trend which is today followed by most psychoanalysts. A trend which leads first to recognition of the analyst's role in the analytic situation and, in this way, to definition of the analytic process less as a *repetition* of the past for which interpretation suffices, than as a *creation* which demands recognition of that which has not occurred' (J.-B. Pontalis, 1978, p. 115).

It is always possible to ask to what extent the successors of any great thinker—be it Plato, Aristotle, Marx or, for us,

Freud—should adhere to the basic premises of the system. There is always some point at which an epistemological rift may occur, resulting in the birth of a *new* idea, little or not at all related to preceding theory. It is this point that may separate an 'old' from a 'new' school of thought. 'Revisionism' begins where old tenets leave off. I have tried to show to what extent Balint worked within the framework of Freud's premises, taking up Freud's fundamental ideas and his instruments of work, and adding his own innovations to them. Each of us will have to decide for himself whether Balint's work is the product of revisionism or fertile development. There is, however, no doubt that for Balint his work was in the spirit of development remaining faithful to Freud and, of course, to Ferenczi. His approach was innovative and has contributed to the renewal of psychoanalytic thought.

NOTES

1. The Congress witnessed Ferenczi's courageous swan song, his paper 'Confusion of Tongues between Adults and the Child' (Ferenczi, 1933 [294]), which some colleagues wanted to prevent being read in public. In a sense it was his last will and testament.
2. In referring to Balint's writings, the year quoted first is that of the original publication. The letter following it identifies individual works of that particular year. The date following the word 'in' indicates the year of publication of the volume in which the work was reprinted (cf. Appendix B).
3. Balint also observed that Ferenczi's contributions are easily forgotten because he raised embarrassing issues.
4. Balint explains the derivation of these two words as follows: 'I propose to coin two new terms. Greek scholars among my readers will know that "acrobat" means literally "he who walks on his toes", i.e. away from the safe earth. Taking this word as my model, I have coined "philobat" to describe one who enjoys such thrills; from which one can easily form the adjective "philobatic" to describe the pleasures and activities, and the abstract noun "philobatism" to describe the whole field. We need another term to describe the apparent opposite of a philobat, one who cannot stand swings and switchbacks, who prefers

to clutch at something firm when his security is in danger. For this I propose "ocnophil", derived from the Greek verb *okneo,* meaning "to shrink, to hesitate, to cling, to hang back". From this word we get the adjective "ocnophilic" and the abstract noun "ocnophilia"' (Balint, 1959a, p. 25).

5. To a certain extent Balint's concept of trauma corresponds to Ferenczi's concept of shock and ensuing disavowal by others (observation made by P. Sabourin).

6. Expression coined by Ferenczi (1932 [308], *FIN.,* p. 279).

7. Written in Hungarian, the notes for this planned article have been translated into French, but not into English or German and are therefore not to be found in the English or German editions of Ferenczi's complete works.

8. Balint had this to say about Searles, Winnicott, Little and Khan: 'All these analysts, including myself, belong—not to the "classical" massive centre—but to the fringe. We are known, tolerated, perhaps even read, but certainly not quoted' (Balint, 1968a, p. 155).

9. Not without irony, he declared that 'the human mind is not essentially different in London from what it is in Vienna or in Budapest' (Balint, 1937b, in 1965a, p. 75). 'The various research workers start from different points of observation and use somewhat different terms. The word "opinion" is used intentionally. We must not forget that we are arguing here about theoretical constructions' (ibid.).

10. These ideas have sometimes been attributed exclusively to D. W. Winnicott.

CHAPTER 6

From Budapest to London: The life of Michael Balint

> The main thing in the life of men resides in what and how they think, and not in what they do or endure.
>
> Albert Einstein in his *Autobiography*

A lthough the diverse and elusive elements that undeniably link a man's life and works are difficult to grasp, I feel, nevertheless, that it is of interest to present Balint's life.

Michael Maurice Balint was born in Budapest on 3 December 1896. His father, Dr. Bergsmann, was a general practitioner in Józsefváros, a section of Budapest populated mainly by small businessmen and called Josefstadt by the German-speaking portion of its inhabitants. Balint spoke of his father as a very good medical practitioner but without scientific ambitions, who seemed somewhat disappointed by the limits of medicine. Balint relates that his father learned Hungarian only in secondary school as a foreign language (letter to O. Dormandi, 3 January 1945), that his paternal grandfather spoke Hungarian fairly well but that his paternal grandmother spoke only German. The family had been fully assimilated Hungarians for only two or three generations.

'It was under Joseph the Second [Emperor of Austria from 1780 to 1790] that in the whole Habsburg Empire the

Jews were compelled to adopt family names for the first time, and naturally most of them had to choose Germanic names. In the nationalistic revival at the end of the nineteenth century, as a reaction against unjustified Germanification in the absolutist period, a very great number of Jews changed their German names by a kind of deed poll to Hungarian names'[1] (Balint in a letter to Ernest Jones, 10 May 1954). Balint himself had his family name legally changed from Bergsmann to Balint, much to his father's dismay. Like many middle-class Hungarian Jews, Balint was converted to the Unitarian faith.

In secondary school he was already a voracious reader and haunted Budapest's public libraries. His sister, Emmi, a year and a half his junior, studied mathematics. She was at school with Margaret Mahler and Alice Székely-Kovacs, Michael's future wife.

He enrolled in medical school at his father's request, as he half-seriously claimed. Soon afterwards, he was called up for military service in the First World War and sent to the front, first in Russia, then in the Italian Dolomites. He was wounded on the thumb, and some suspected that he may have mutilated himself in order to get out of the army, whereas others reported that his innate curiosity got the better of him and he was injured while attempting to dismantle a hand grenade. In any event, he was able to return to his studies after two and a half years. He literally fell in love with chemistry and plunged enthusiastically into the study of biochemistry and physics. By October 1918, shortly after the 'Aster Revolution', he had completed his medical studies.[2] Although a medical student, he attended the courses on psychoanalysis given in 1919 by Ferenczi, who was the first university professor of psychoanalysis in the world. This was his first contact with Ferenczi. Balint recalls his conversion to psychoanalysis in the preface to one of his books. 'After having highly ambivalently criticized *The Interpretation of Dreams* and *The Psychopathology of Everyday Life*, I was at the age of 21 decisively and definitely conquered for psycho-analysis by the *Three Essays* and *Totem and Taboo*. In some form or other these two directions of research—the development of the individual sexual function and the development of human relations—have remained in the focus of my interest ever since' (Balint, 1952a, p. vii). He attended a seminar on Freud's 'Studies on Hysteria' given in Budapest by Sandor Rado.

> [In] 1917, *Totem and Taboo* was lent to me by a young girl who was then studying pure mathematics. ... We married soon after I had finished my medical studies, and a few months later started our analytic training with Dr. H. Sachs in Berlin on the same day. After some time both of us changed over to Ferenczi, and we finished our training under him. Starting with our shared enthusiasm for *Totem and Taboo* till her death in 1939, Alice and I read, studied, lived and worked together. All our ideas—no matter in whose mind they had first arisen— were enjoyed and then tested, probed and criticized in our endless discussions. Quite often it was just chance that decided which of us should publish a particular idea. Apart from psycho-analysis, Alice's main interests were anthropology and education, mine biology and medicine, and usually this factor decided who should write about the idea. We published only one paper jointly, although almost all of them could have been printed under our joint names. In fact, our development was ... intertwined' (ibid., pp. vii–viii).

His marriage to Alice was extremely harmonious. They were an inseparable couple, living and working together in a way that he subsequently re-created in his marriage with Enid Eichholz, born Albu, which took place in London in 1953.

As we know from Hermann's Mémoirs, Balint was forced, 'after the overthrow of Béla Kun's Communist Republic early in August of 1919', to seek refuge in the university apartment of a professor. 'We had become', Hermann writes, 'the target of a few counterrevolutionary and racist factions of the "Hungarian Reawakening" movement' (Hermann, 1974, p. 45 of French edition).

Because of the uncertain political situation in Budapest, Balint and his wife decided to live in Berlin. At first he was an assistant in the biochemical laboratory of Otto Warburg, a future Nobel prize winner (1931). Alice pursued studies and research at the Museum of Ethnology, while Michael worked half-time at the Berlin Psychoanalytic Institute, where he conducted psychoanalytic treatment, an activity he continued for the rest of his life. After obtaining his Ph.D. in biochemistry, he began to treat psychosomatic cases at Berlin's Charité Hospital, and was thus the first man in history to analyse such cases.[3]

At that time Karl Abraham was president of the Berlin Institute and Max Eitingon director of the treatment center. Melanie Klein had already been at the Berlin Institute for some time. As a sidelight to history, it is reported that Balint first met Melanie Klein in Ferenczi's waiting room in Budapest. Balint found other compatriots at Berlin—Rado and Harnik, for example. Subsequently Helene Deutsch came to Berlin from her native Vienna. Balint recalled the atmosphere of that period as being very stimulating. However, he was less satisfied with his personal analysis, which he felt was too akin to a teaching experience, even an indoctrination. He and Alice therefore decided, in 1924, to return to Budapest to continue their analyses with Ferenczi. Michael's first analysis with Sachs had lasted two years. The second also lasted two years until Ferenczi left Hungary at the end of 1926 to spend eight months in New York. It was at this point that Balint began to feel he was truly an analyst. His metamorphosis is reflected in the trend of his publications during that period: from 1924 to 1926, he wrote on bacteriology and chemistry; from 1925 on, he published articles on psychoanalysis.

Back in Budapest, he spent two years as research assistant in one of the Departments of Medicine at the University Hospital.

Figure 5. Alice Balint (family photograph).

After returning to Budapest in 1924, I asked Professor Koranyi to allow me to continue this work [of psychosomatic medicine] in his Clinic. ... He eventually agreed in principle to my request, but the practical difficulties proved so great that my plans had to be given up.

For a while L. Friedrich offered me facilities in his Gastroenterological Department. Although this collaboration seemed most promising, in the end the practical difficulties proved overwhelming; for instance, the only room available for psychotherapy was the X-ray cabinet, a small dark room with no windows and cluttered with strange apparatus. As my analytic practice developed and claimed more and more of my time, I decided not to continue the struggle for the time being' (Balint, 1970c, p. 457).

Nevertheless, he resumed this work later in his life in London, after he had emigrated to England.

He soon became a member of the Hungarian Psychoanalytical Society.[4] From 1931 to 1935 he was vice-director of the Budapest Psychoanalytic Institute (of which Ferenczi had been the first director in 1930), and, finally, director from 1935 to 1939.

He played an important part in the establishment in 1930 of the Psychoanalytic Out-patient Clinic where more patients were treated at the time than in Vienna or Berlin. The Clinic was not officially subsidized and was supported exclusively by private donations and the professional activity of members of the Hungarian Society.

The Clinic was located at Number 12 Mészáros Street in a house 'frequented by Imre Hermann, Michael Balint, Sigmund Pfeiffer, Ladislas Révész, Robert Bak, Géza Dukész, Mrs. Robert Felszeghy, Edith Gyömröi, Lili Hajdu, Géza Róheim' (Farkashazy, 1982). The Balints lived on the fourth floor of the building, which was owned by Frederick Kovacs, its architect. Kovacs was the second husband of Vilma Kovacs, Alice Balint's mother. Herself an analyst, Vilma published, in 1936, a remarkable article on psychoanalytic training entitled 'Training and Control-analysis' (quoted in Chapter 4). Frederick Kovacs was like a generous pater familias to the group. A hard-working man who had achieved middle-class status, he lived in Naphegy, on the right bank of the capital. In 1930 Ferenczi fulfilled his long-time ambition to live in Buda and bought a house in Naphegy, where he was a frequent guest in the Kovacs home and associated with the many artists and intellectuals who were received there. The Kovacs home was burned down at the end of the Second World War.

Michael Balint was a sportsman. He rowed on the Danube, ice-skated in Budapest's Municipal Park and skied in the outskirts of the city, and, as was customary for the Hungarian bourgeoisie of that time, he spent a month every year on holiday in Tragors (Austria) with the whole family and with friends.

When the young army officer Gömbös seized power in 1932, the Hungarian government took on the trappings of a racist, pro-Hitlerian state. The police had to be notified of every meeting and seminar held by the Hungarian Psychoanalytical Society. The political atmosphere became grimmer by the day. Balint speaks of it as follows:

in the thirties ... the political situation in Hungary became tenser every day. It seemed most unlikely that any institution could offer me facilities for testing out my ideas so I decided to gather a few general practitioners in a kind of seminar for the study of psychotherapeutic possibilities in their practice. Although I had only vague ideas of what was needed by my colleagues—e.g. I started the seminars with a series of lectures, which I know now are quite useless—the interest remained alive and even a second group was formed. However, the political situation deteriorated further; we were ordered to notify the police of every one of our meetings with the result that a plain-clothes policeman attended each of them, taking copious notes of everything that was said. We could never find out what these notes contained or who read them.

Figure 6.   Alice and Michael Balint (family photograph).

The only result we knew of was that on several occasions the detective, after the meeting, consulted one of us either about himself, his wife, or his children. This was quite amusing for us, but no proper discussions could develop under these circumstances and the group of doctors disintegrated eventually (Balint, 1970c, p. 458, English from the original dactyloscript).

In his formative years, Balint was surrounded by artists and intellectuals and was immersed in Budapest's flourishing cultural life (cf. Chapter 3). He was friendly with the painter Robert Berényi, with Leo Wiener, the composer and musicologist, with Grete Varo, who set up a music academy in Budapest and later in Chicago, and with the artist Rippl-Ronay. After he became an analyst, Balint made friends among his colleagues, like Istvan Hollós. However, he considered Géza Róheim and Otto Fenichel his closest friends. He and Fenichel, who belonged to the group that has been called 'the Freudian left' (see Jacoby, 1983), engaged in a lively exchange of ideas on such subjects as the importance of the social context in psychoanalytic understanding. Balint liked the confrontation of ideas in the form of either very lively discussions or in correspondence.

After the Austrian Anschluss, Freud and his family found refuge in England. The Balints followed suit. Balint requested the aid of Ernest Jones and John Rickman. Michael, Alice and their son John arrived in Manchester, England, where they took up residence at 1 Mayfair Cottage in Fielden Park at the beginning of 1939.

It was there that Alice died suddenly, on 29 August 1939. Michael wrote how, on the 27th of August, they went for a Sunday stroll, paid a call on friends and rejoiced over the development of possibilities for work in their newly adopted country. The next day, Alice was visiting a friend when she lost consciousness. Michael came to fetch her, and she was put to bed with gastrointestinal symptoms. Her doctor was called in. The following morning, Alice fainted again while she was combing her hair, and when her physician arrived, he could only record her death. She died of a ruptured aneurysm at the age of forty. Both Michael and she had been aware of that anomaly and had lived in the shadow of her possible sudden death.

Michael Balint continued to live in Manchester, where he was appointed psychiatric consultant at the Manchester Northern Royal Hospital, and director of two child guidance centres: The North East Lancashire Child Guidance Clinic (1944) and the County Borough of Preston Child Guidance Clinic (1945). From 1945 to 1947 he directed The Chislehurst Child Guidance Clinic.

After obtaining British medical qualifications, he wrote a thesis on individual differences in infants and received a Master of Science degree in psychology from the University of Manchester. One of his discoveries was that infants have constant but individual natural feeding rhythms. His study was a forerunner of a type of research that was to become quite fashionable.[5]

In July 1944, Michael remarried. He and his second wife, Edna Oakeshott, separated in March of 1947 (Sutherland, 1971, p. 331), although they were not officially divorced until 1952. He went through a very difficult time until 1953, when he married Enid Flora Eichholz, née Albu.

In 1945 Michael Balint was notified of his parents' death. They had committed suicide when they were about to be arrested by the Hungarian Nazis. On 15 January 1945 he wrote to Alice's sister, Olga Dormandi, 'It is true that I had neglected my father for a long time. We never got along too well. We were never really on good terms. But I inherited my intelligence, my logical mind, my capacity for work from him. I loved my mother very much. She was so in touch with life; things never worked out well for her and still she never gave up hope'. Some think that Balint's interest in training general practitioners in psychotherapy stemmed from a desire to improve general medical practice, but that it was ultimately a particular desire to help his father in his medical practice.

In 1946 the British Psychoanalytical Society decided to send an envoy to Budapest to renew professional contact. Michael Balint was elected for the task. The journey through post-war Europe to a Hungary in ruins must have been a painful one for him.

In October 1945 he moved to London, living first at New Grove House in Hampstead Grove, then in Devonshire Place. He became a British subject in October 1947. From that time onward, he practised psychoanalysis.[6] At the same time, while working as a consultant at the Tavistock Clinic, he became interested in group work. Like his mentor Ferenczi before him, he conducted experiments in human relations. His experiments bore on ways and means to sensitize doctors to unconscious interactions with their patients. His purpose was to use psychoanalytic insights to improve psychotherapeutic interventions. He dealt with the same problem that had confronted Sándor Ferenczi and Franz Alexander: to ascertain whether analytically oriented psychotherapy is possible and, if so, under what conditions. He published abundantly on the subject, either alone or in collaboration with Enid Balint and, subsequently, with P. Ornstein. One of these publications, a book on focal psychotherapy (Balint, 1972a), shows how Balint worked; in it, he gives a detailed account of one of the cases he treated.

From the time of his arrival in England in 1939, Balint re-established a circle of friends among the Hungarian emigré community, which included Paul Ignotus (the son of the Hungarian Poet Hugo Ignotus, one of Ferenczi's friends), the historian and journalist, author of the best history of Hungary to be written by a Hungarian expatriate in the British capital. The community also included Louis Kentner, concert pianist and author of a book on music,[7] who was married to the sister of Yehudi Menuhin's wife.

Balint also maintained close ties with his non-Hungarian colleagues. His closest professional associate in London was John Rickman (Bion's first analyst). Balint particularly enjoyed his long discussions with John Rickman, who had undergone an analysis with Ferenczi to which Jones had been privy (Masson, 1984, p. 173). He saw much of Ernest Jones. Despite their professional differences of opinion, he counted Melanie Klein among his friends. Anna Freud also thought of herself as a friend. He spent his leisure time with the Sandler family and with W. Joffe. He was good friends with John D. Sutherland and his family. His professional associates included Tom Main, Max Clyne, Michael Courtenay, Cyril H. Gill and many more. He maintained relations with numerous friends abroad: with Dr. Morris Levine and his family as well as with colleagues Paul and Anna Ornstein in Cincinnati, who had been very hospitable to him when he was visiting professor there; with the Raimbaults, the Gendrauts and Michel Sapir in Paris; with Boris Luban-Plozza in Switzerland, and with many others.

Figure 7.   Enid and Michael Balint at the beginning of the 1960s
(photograph by Mrs. Burke).

Between 1948 and 1961, Balint worked at the Tavistock
Clinic. For the first dozen years after its foundation in 1920,
the Clinic had devoted its efforts chiefly toward the
introduction of psychotherapeutic methods for patients
suffering from psychoneurosis and allied complaints (Dicks,
1970; Gosling, 1966). Around 1932, the Tavistock staff
began to devote more and more of its time to imparting
psychological knowledge and skills to other professional
workers of many backgrounds. Gradually, the staffs of the
Clinic and of the Tavistock Institute of Human Relations, a
newly founded associate organization, became intensely
interested in developing the structure and functioning of
training groups (cf. Bion). They extended their scope to the
study of natural groups such as couples and families.

In 1947, Balint's future wife Enid was working for the
Family Welfare Association. She requested help from the

Tavistock Institute of Human Relations and the Tavistock Clinic in developing techniques for assisting people in marital difficulties and in developing methods of training in the use of these techniques. A seminar for social workers was formed in 1948, and this became the Family Discussion Bureau.

Early in 1949, when Balint came to the Tavistock Clinic, he was asked to join the project. Together, Enid and Michael developed the 'case discussion seminar', which still remains one of the key elements of the program of the Institute of Marital Studies, successor to the Family Discussion Bureau. Enid Balint was the founder and moving spirit of the latter. It was for this group of social workers that she and Michael Balint worked out the training program later adapted to meet training needs for general practitioners. From its inception, she took part in the new undertaking, first as a co-leader and case supervisor, then as the leader of a research seminar for general practitioners. The format they developed for their seminar was subsequently adopted for basic psychological training in a number of other professions.

Later, Michael Balint organized 'Research cum Training' seminars for general practitioners wishing to get a better understanding of the emotional problems they encountered in their everyday practice. This activity was not new to him. Prior to 1939, he had successfully engaged in this kind of training in Budapest following Ferenczi's example (as we now know from the Freud–Ferenczi correspondence). In the autumn of 1950, he launched his first seminar for general practitioners in London, and he continued this activity for the rest of his life.

Simultaneously, he practised psychoanalysis for at least six hours a day. After his retirement from the Tavistock Clinic in 1961 he joined the staff of University College Hospital in London. In this capacity, he not only conducted seminars for general practitioners, but also adapted his methods to the training of medical students, an activity he pursued until 1968. He was pleased with his academic

Figure 8.   Michael Balint (drawing, 1970, by O. Dormandi).

achievements, proud of being a full professor in London, just as he was proud of his son's professorship in the United States. He was, moreover, visiting professor in Cincinnati, Ohio, and President of the Medical Section of the British Psychological Society. He held several offices in the British Psychoanalytical Society: he was Scientific Secretary from 1951 to 1953 and President from 1968 to his sudden death on 31 December 1970. It was his idea to hold the Franco–British Conferences and his responsibility to organize them. As President of the British Society, he initiated the London Conferences for English-speaking members of the European Societies.

Balint travelled widely on the Continent. He lectured and taught in Paris and Switzerland. He even returned to Germany, where he toiled with others to build the new

Figure 9.   Enid Balint (drawing, 1970, by O. Dormandi).

German psychoanalysis (Mitscherlich and Loch had been his analysands in London). During the 1920s, he had spent time in the pre-Hitlerian Berlin under the Weimar Republic, and his return in the post-war years must have awakened nostalgic memories of those intellectually exhilarating days in the former German capital.

Enid and Michael Balint worked closely together. They co-authored a number of books: *Psychotherapeutic Techniques in Medicine* (1961a), some in collaboration with other authors such as *A Study of Doctors* (1966a) with Gosling and Hildebrand, or *Focal Psychotherapy*[8] (1972a) with Ornstein. After Michael's death, Enid collaborated with J. S. Norrell to produce a study on interactions in general medical practice entitled *Six Minutes for the Patient* (1973).

Even the purely psychoanalytic book on regression

written by Michael includes chapters and case material by Enid. In a 1968 paper entitled 'What Is Psychoanalysis?'— part of a series of public lectures sponsored by the British Psychoanalytical Society—Enid speaks of 'unconscious communications between husband and wife'. She says, 'Perhaps marriage somehow goes beyond the natural field of interest of the psychoanalyst whose main field of interest is the individual alone—his urges and drives and his relation to his own private life which include his dreams and fantasies, his hopes, disappointments and wishes, about his family as he first knew—or imagined he knew them' (E. Balint, 1968, p. 40). This brief quotation is characteristic of her style. All her personal research goes beyond 'the natural field of interest' of psychoanalysis and is perhaps so fascinating for this very reason. Psychoanalysis is ever-present in Enid Balint's work, a tool for understanding the couple, the family and the doctor–patient relationship. At the same time, her work remains faithful to the spirit of the important twentieth-century discoveries in this field: intuition on the one hand, work and methodology on the other. The unconscious does not yield its secrets readily. It is an arduous path that leads to discovery. Freud spoke of 'working through' [Durcharbeiten], 'the work of mourning' [Trauerarbeit], 'elaboration' [Verarbeitung] and 'dream work' [Traumarbeit]. In the Balints' writings, scientific work and methodology bear the indelible trace of the best in Freudian tradition. One of the aims of the seminars was to discover and to use the capacity for change in the participants. That important but limited change of personality Michael spoke of depends largely on the motivation of the members of the seminars.

'Training as an Impetus to Ego Development' (1967) is the significant title of one of Enid Balint's works. The analyst, like the doctor, is constantly developing. The training is there so that this development can take place in contact with his professional work. 'Fair Shares and Mutual Concern' (1972) is another evocative article describing group work with general practitioners and social workers.

The processes of identification are the pivot for emotional learning, but must not become dependency. Is this perhaps one of the main lessons to be learned from Balints' work?

Enid's writings typically shuttle back and forth between clinical observation and theory. They contain none of the smug philosophical musings, devoid of clinical material, none of the ambitious will to 'set the world on fire', that characterize certain post-Freudian trends.

When dealing with the subject of the 'doctor as a drug', she leads doctors to question themselves, to ask what they bring to their patients and how they can become dangerous, like 'drugs'—in other words, questioning the counter-transference, the role of the doctor in the doctor–patient relationship. Enid writes:

I train not only general practitioners but also psychoanalysts, and I am always amazed to note how difficult it is for psychoanalysts in training, or in supervision, who are, moreover, qualified psychiatrists, to understand what their patients are trying to communicate. When I began supervising, I thought it was impossible that such well trained, experienced doctors, who had undergone analysis, read Freud widely, and attended lectures and seminars, could not understand what would seem to the experienced analyst to be quite simple communications, easy to interpret to the patient. Clearly, we must bear in mind that it is always easy to understand someone else's material, and always difficult to understand material presented to us directly by the patient. Even so, over the years I have become convinced that nothing can replace clinical experience and that clinical experience alone will not lead to better understanding unless it is combined with the type of training developed by Michael Balint' (E. Balint, 1973, p. 17).

Michael Balint's famous book *The Doctor, His Patient and the Illness* (1957a) was published in Hungarian in 1961—the first psychoanalytic work to be published in

Figure 10.   Caricature by Stern & Stern from a felicitation document addressed to M. Balint for his 70th birthday, 3 December 1966.

Hungary after the Stalin era. Although it was attacked as 'bourgeois' when it appeared, in that same year Balint returned to Budapest, where he was acclaimed by the Hungarian Medical Academy, by his editors and by his colleagues, perhaps for the first time in his native land. It was of course a generation that had grown up since he had left the country and therefore had not known him.

Balint seemed to be in good health in spite of a mild form of diabetes, which required no treatment other than diet. In the final years of his life, however, he suffered from glaucoma, which necessitated two operations. He had a first myocardial infarction in 1955, a second in December of 1970

Figure 11. Caricature by Stern & Stern from a felicitation document addressed to M. Balint for his 70th birthday, 3 December 1966.

at the age of 74. He recovered, but two weeks after leaving the hospital, he died suddenly (probably of acute ventricular fibrillation).

His kindness, his humanity, his understanding, his compassion and his aversion for authoritarian relationships or dependency were equalled only by his independent spirit. His belief that psychoanalysis should progress through the contributions of independent thinkers and an uncompromising desire for truth, and that it constitutes an important contribution to the understanding of mankind, made him feel that it was one of the most significant fields *in the service* of man and mankind. As a result, he was saddened

Figure 12.   Michael Balint (photograph by E. Stein).

by the pettiness of some persons engaged in psychoanalytic research. He believed that psychoanalysis had an important calling, both as a science and as a method. He was convinced that his contribution to the understanding of the exchanges between the doctor and his patient brought *psychoanalysis* to an important sphere of human activity: Medicine. In his research, he felt that as a *psychoanalyst* he played his part in the understanding and clarification of human relations.

Balint was a hard worker and a voracious reader. He read everything he could get his hands on, from philosophy to thrillers. He lived as intensely as he loved. He sometimes flew into a rage. He could be scornful or maladroit and was often provocative, an iconoclast. He enjoyed wit. He had intense vitality, a need to love and be loved, real zeal for science and research. In the English social atmosphere he could pass for 'the Hungarian savage'. A man of huge proportions, he could, through self-control, present a gentle and moderate bearing in his professional life. This apparently mild attitude stood him in good stead in the conflicts over both Ferenczi's work and his own application of psychoanalysis to the doctor and his patient. For some, this was a 'cheapening of psychoanalysis', for others his concepts were 'too psychoanalytical'. It was his independence of spirit that enabled him to stand up under such controversies.

He had a smooth style, not devoid of humour and provocation. His immense curiosity encompassed both the miraculous cures in Lourdes (Balint, 1955a, in 1956a, p. 194) and the Szondi test (Balint, 1948c, in 1956a, p. 261). He knew how to awaken the interest of his pupils, but they never left a supervision 'feeling indoctrinated' (Joffe, 1971). He inspired rather than taught.

Balint was not active in politics, although several labour members of parliament belonged to his circle of friends. In the general enthusiasm following the War, he was in favour of the reorganization of medicine under the National Health Service, even though, like most physicians, particularly of his generation, he had a certain aversion for decisions on health made by non-medical government officials.

A free thinker, Michael Balint also maintained cultural ties with the traditional institutions of his native land, but despite that, it is surprising to hear him quote, at the end of his speech at the 1953 London Congress, the motto of the Unitarian Church of Hungary, which ought to be the motto of training regulations too: *'semper reformari debet'* [reform unremittingly] (Balint, 1965a, p. 285).

Balint's followers primarily came from the British Middle Group. However, they also included those whom Cremerius described as the spiritual descendants of

Ferenczi (Cremerius, 1983, p. 1004); apart from Winnicott, they include a list of such diverse personalities as Masud Khan, Margaret Mahler, Margaret Little, Wilfred Bion, René Spitz, Sacha Nacht, Heinz Kohut, Donald Meltzer, Harold Searles and others.

Balint was both indulgent towards his colleagues and demanding of them. He claimed that psychoanalysis was full of promise, provided that psychoanalysts could see beyond the four walls of their consulting-rooms. At the same time, in line with Ferenczi's views, he considered that it is discoveries made by applying psychoanalytic *methods* that are the most important in the field, not speculations remote from clinical observation.

Finally, he did not belong to any group, political or professional, and for this reason he was in a position, as Professor at University College Hospital and as President of his Psychoanalytical Society, to promote integration. He belonged only to himself.

NOTES

1. This was part of a long-range national policy aimed at assimilating minorities. In 1850, 56% of Hungary's inhabitants claimed German as their mother tongue, whereas only 36% claimed Hungarian; in 1880, 56% claimed Hungarian and only 34% German; in 1900, 85% Hungarian and only 9.4% German. 'Magyarization was in full swing, and yesterday's Germans and Jews became champions of the national movement' (Molnar, 1985).

2. Balint did not receive his diploma until 1924.

3. A professor of biochemistry at Berlin's Charité Hospital who was of Hungarian extraction, Peter Rona, recommended Ferenczi to two of his fellow faculty members: Wilhelm His and Zondeck, Professor of Internal Medicine. Balint's acquaintanceship with these two influential physicians was a determining factor in his life, for it was through them that he was allowed to treat psychosomatic patients at the Charité.

4. Contrary to some reports in his biographies, Balint was never president of the Hungarian Psychoanalytical Society.

5. René Spitz and Margaret Mahler, pioneers in this field, were both, like Balint, products of the Budapest school.

6. It is not surprising to find that the first paper Balint read before the British Society dealt with 'transference'.
7. Kentner, L. (1976), *Piano*, Paris: Hatier, 1978.
8. *Focal Psychotherapy* bears the subtitle: *An Example of Applied Psychoanalysis*.

CHAPTER SEVEN

An emerging perspective of controversies

> Culture is activity of thought, and receptiveness to beauty and human feeling.
>
> Alfred North Whitehead, *The Aims of Education*

> Convictions are more dangerous foes of truth than lies.
>
> Friedrich Nietzsche, *Human, All Too Human*

It is widely known that Freud *created* the analytic situation from hypnosis, according to his personality. For instance he said: 'I cannot put up with being stared at by other people for eight hours a day (or more)' (Freud, 1913c, *12*:134). And then, there is a permanent tension, one feels, between his interest in understanding the Other, and the need for a methodological research with a view to the therapeutic outcome. One such example is his way of terminating the 'Wolf Man's' analysis (Freud, 1918b). 'Our technique grew up in the treatment of hysteria ... but the phobias have already made it necessary to go beyond our former limits' (Freud, 1919a [1918], *17*:165). As this search for sound technique necessarily involved a series of trials and errors, Freud did not take it up. It was Ferenczi who devoted special attention to the question; probably in part because he was dissatisfied with his own analysis and more eager than Freud to cure patients, he became engrossed, towards the end of the first decade of the century, in seeking ways to transform the field of analysis according to his own desire for provoking changes. He continued this activity

127

until his death in 1933. In the process he became critical of Freud, as their correspondence shows. Freud was not always the ideal analyst Ferenczi would have wished, and at times he even had the feeling that Freud wanted to prevent his becoming one.

This controversy was painful for both men, as well as for analysts who were witness to their disagreements. After an unproductive period, which Balint believed was due to a genuine 'traumatism' (Balint, 1968a, p. 207), analysts began to work towards a better understanding of the analytic setting and process. It was in line with this trend that Michael and Alice Balint made their greatest contributions, especially in their 1939 article on counter-transference (Balint & Balint, 1939a). More particularly, Michael Balint took up the whole question Ferenczi had raised about the significance of regression, the archaic moulds of the analytic relationship (cf. his concepts of 'ocnophilia' and 'philobatism'), and of the mutual interactions between transference and counter-transference, the cornerstone of his research. In parallel to the thinking of another of Ferenczi's pupils, Melanie Klein, Balint's work in this field produced new ideas that made it possible for such outstanding authors as Donald Winnicott and Paula Heimann to rethink analytic technique.

Representing analysis as an empirical science in which the scientist—the analyst—investigated his subject—the analysand—with complete neutrality, Freud declared that the central issue in psychoanalysis was transference. Records of his practice, however, prove that he did not act accordingly. Moreover, he rather favoured interpretations that took patients back to their past. The part played by the analyst and the setting were not included in this interpretative approach. It was Ferenczi who first emphasized that analysis is 'a social fact' (Ferenczi, 1985, p. 36). In the course of his 'experiments' he discovered the importance of a non-intrusive atmosphere, created by the analyst, to provide the psychological conditions for the cooperative effort that promotes productive analytic work. Balint considered the psychoanalytic *consequences* of *different techniques*—for example, fostering idealization and dependency. Such investigations gave a real awareness of the nature of the analytic situation and the quality of the relationship it promotes. Systematic consideration of the counter-transference in the broad sense of the word was recommended by Ferenczi and is now widely recognized by his followers. Ferenczi coined the term 'introjection' and investigated the basic nature of the psychological phenomenon to which it refers: the mechanism by which the mind is shaped. The concepts of introjection and projection have become useful tools for understanding the dynamics of the exchanges between the analysand and the analyst.

The modifications made to analytic listening expanded its focus to include not only what the analysand expresses *but also* what the analyst feels, to include the *role* of the analyst and the analytic setting, and the understanding of *regression* as an opportunity for 'new beginning'—a more ambitious objective than mere reconstruction of the past. This made it legitimate to ask whether there were not just one, but rather *two types* of psychoanalysis: the first, paternal, rational, based on memory and insight—the classical one; the other more maternal, regressive, based on interaction, experience, the non-verbal—more 'profound'. Such a dichotomy belongs to a pattern of thought that refers to binary systems where automatically the one is the 'good'—us—the other the 'bad'—the others. Schematic typology, however, obscures the fact that there are many *analytic styles,* according to the different sensitivities, education and cultural backgrounds of individual analysts. It would be an oversimplification to say that there are as many analytic styles as there are analysts. However, since the survey carried out by Glover at the end of the 1930s (Glover, 1940), it has not been possible to cling to the illusion that there can be one *standard* form of analytic practice. Despite this inevitable diversity of styles, it is possible to define an *ultimate goal* for psychoanalysis as the expansion of the field of consciousness by reintegrating

Figure 13. The Hungarian Psychoanalytical Group, July 1928, on the occasion of the 55th birthday of Ferenczi (Juca Gimes, Zurich).

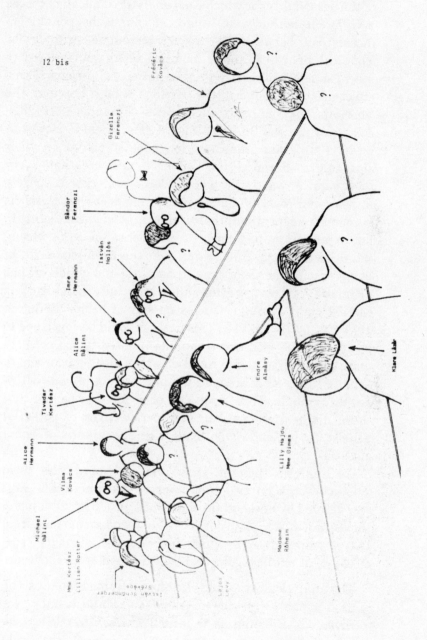

what was unconscious—the personal growth and liberation of the personality for which each analytic couple may choose a *different pathway*. It would, of course, be possible to distinguish between a classical technique suitable for 'classical neuroses' and a modified technique tailored to meet the needs of more regressed patients. Passages to this effect are to be found in the writings of both Ferenczi, the 'specialist in peculiarly difficult cases' (Ferenczi, 1931 [292], *FIN.*, p. 128), and Balint (Balint, 1968a, passim). However, quite a different interpretation can be placed on their statements. Ferenczi, for instance, affirms that every analysand ('even those who undergo analysis for purely professional reasons'!), can benefit from deeper analysis. 'It becomes evident, then, that even character formation is to be regarded as a remote consequence of very strong infantile traumas. But I think that the cathartic result of being submerged for a time in neurosis and childhood has ultimately an invigorating effect and that, if the work is carried right through, it does no sort of harm' (Ferenczi, 1931 [292], *FIN.*, p. 141). This passage could be construed to mean that the modified technique tailored to the needs of more regressed patients could also be used to advantage to explore interesting areas in the unconscious of less regressed individuals. This is roughly equivalent to saying that these discoveries open up new perspectives of potential benefit to patients 'who have the appearance of being classical'.

As analytic thought grew and developed, the term 'classical' took on two superimposed meanings. The *first* was defined by Ferenczi (Freud, 1965a, p. 346) in alluding to the technical rules laid down by Freud and, in particular, to the recommendation—which he, Ferenczi, strongly criticized—that analysts adopt a receptive, non-active attitude.

The analytical situation—i.e. the restrained coolness, the professional hypocrisy and—hidden behind it but never revealed—a dislike of the patient which, nevertheless, he felt in all his being—such a situation was not essentially different from that which in his childhood had led to the illness. When, in addition to the strain caused by the analytical situation, we imposed on the patient the further burden of reproducing the original trauma, we created a situation that was indeed unbearable. Small wonder that our effort produced no better results than the original trauma. The setting free of his critical feelings, the willingness on our part to admit our mistakes and the honest endeavour to avoid them in future, all these go to create in the patient a confidence in the analyst. *It is this confidence that establishes the contrast between the present and the unbearable traumatogenic past,* the contrast which is absolutely necessary for the patient in order to enable him to re-experience the past no longer as hallucinatory reproduction but as an objective memory. Suppressed criticisms felt by my patients, e.g. the discovery, with uncanny clairvoyance, of the aggressive features of my 'active therapy', of the professional hypocrisy in the forcing of relaxation, taught me to recognize and to control the exaggerations in both directions (Ferenczi, 1933 [294], *FIN.*, pp. 159–160 [italics in the original]).

The *second* meaning of the term 'classical' stems from a tacit consensus reached by analysts at the end of the 1930s. In this sense it is used to designate a non-interventionist, non-active analytic technique. By this definition the technique recommended by the school of Melanie Klein would be considered too 'active' to be 'classical'. Classical technique therefore consists in *strict* non-interference by the analyst and more-or-less exclusive focus on the interpretation of transference. One area, however, remains undefined: it has never been stated how much extra-transference activity may be included in a 'classical' analysis. Although it is actually post-classical, what has come to be known as classical technique refers explicitly to the codification of technique based on Freud's writings or, to be more specific, on the interpretations placed on Freud's technical papers by the psychoanalytic mainstream of the 1940s. At the time the majority of the members of the International Psychoanalytical Association lived in North America, so that the psychoanalytic mainstream of that period could be equated with psychoanalytic trends then prevalent there. The notion of 'parameters' (Eissler, 1953) was used to indicate what deviation was permissible or tolerable in classical analysis as thus defined. This conception of 'classical' analysis was challenged by the schools of thought inspired more or less directly by Ferenczi—that is to say, by the English Middle Group, or the so-called Independents gathered around Balint and Winnicott, and by Melanie Klein and her followers. Subsequently efforts were made to arrive at a clearer understanding of counter-transference. In 1947 Winnicott investigated 'hate in the counter-transference' and stressed the need for regressed patients to feel the true affects of their analyst, including intense negative feelings. In 1950 Paula Heimann pointed out how important it is for analysts to recognize and work through their own feelings toward their analysands. In 1959, Racker attempted to define specific types of feelings analysands provoke in analysts. He distinguished between *identical* and *complementary* feelings. In the first case, the analyst experiences the same feelings as the analysand. In the second case, the analyst experiences the emotions of another person symbolically present (see also Sandler, 1976). If the analyst recognizes identical counter-transference within himself, he should be alerted to a narcissistic type of transference in the analysand; if he becomes aware of complementary counter-transference, he should be alerted to transference patterned after the analysand's archaic object relations.

In the author's opinion, this brief historical review of the issues sheds considerable light on what is currently at stake, for these more recent trends in psychoanalysis spring directly from the controversy between Freud and Ferenczi. Personal frictions and rivalries, of course, also occur in other fields, but in comparison to them the controversy between Freud and Ferenczi was particularly heated. Its tragic impact may have been due to the special professional circumstances surrounding it, to the special bonds that are inevitably established between a leader and his disciple, between an analyst and his analysand in the course of analytic training. Such intense relations are not the rule in other fields, with the possible exception of the fine arts—and in philosophy in antiquity—where, for example, schools of painting and sculpture were created during the Renaissance. Such an intimacy is reinforced by the revelation, in analysis, of innermost thoughts and feelings, and by the fact that the analyst's tool of work—like the artist's—is himself.[1]

One interpretation frequently placed on controversies of this kind may be formulated as follows: those who disagree with the precepts of the *Master* are acting out their resistances. This implies that they are 'at fault' for not recognizing 'the truth'. In psychoanalysis, it is obvious that important discoveries have been made—paradoxically— against resistances that arose in open opposition to attempts at understanding the workings of the mind. But the unwritten law that anyone espousing an idea contradictory to standard credo would be considered 'guilty until proven otherwise' deprived many with original ideas of the means of argument. Nothing indicates that Freud was trying to communicate, 'You view me as the father and your subjective image of me makes it more difficult for you to behave rationally toward me.' On the contrary, Freud often appeared, rather, to affirm, 'I am the father'. Jung openly accused Freud of this tactic. 'You go around sniffing out all the symptomatic actions in your vicinity, thus reducing everyone to the level of children who blushingly admit the existence of their faults' (Freud, 1974, p. 535). Freud responded with, 'I do not deny that I like to be right. All in all, that is a sad privilege, since it is conferred by age' (ibid., p. 476). At the same time, he stayed outside analysis: 'I *no longer* have any need to uncover my personality completely, and you correctly traced this back to the traumatic reason for it. Since Fliess's case ... that need has been extinguished' (letter from Freud to Ferenczi, 6 October 1910, quoted by Jones, 1955, p. 92). Jung felt that Freud had abused psychoanalysis to belittle others and their achievements.[2] In this area of resistance Freud, and some of his followers, too, reserved the right to say what psychoanalysis was and what it was not. 'Adler's [movement is] radically false ...' (Freud, 1914d, *14*:60).

As Vilma Kovacs observed in a 1936 article, vehement disagreements within the movement were first publicly aired at the 1913 Munich Congress. At that meeting Freud felt it was necessary to set the record straight by declaring that he 'did not recognize the innovations of the Swiss as legitimate continuations and further developments of the psycho-analysis that originated with me' (ibid.). This is, then, how matters stood at the time: if Freud approved, it was psychoanalysis; if he disapproved, it was not.[3]

The situation was considerably more complex than a simple difference of opinion between Freud and his followers; there were ties *between psychoanalysts* within the group, which played a part. Rivalries and different temperaments were inevitable. Most of the members of the international movement were recruited from *minority groups*. In Vienna it was made up mainly of Jews from Eastern Europe; in the United States, mainly of immigrants; and everywhere, women were highly influential in a society dominated by men. What was accepted as established fact by the 'compact majority', of which Freud spoke so ironically (Freud, 1925d, *20*:8), was challenged by a fringe group, which, contrary to the majority, was inclined to ask questions and to develop its own ideas. The results could be seen as a 'cultural advance', and it was an element that could create surprise in interpretation. When the meaning of the Oedipus complex had become common knowledge, analysts had to turn to other aspects of the unconscious in order to suprise their analysands.[4] The 'cultural advance', however, is only one aspect of the analyst's 'personal growth'—i.e. of his ever-increasing awareness of his own unconscious—and it is by continuing this process that the analyst remains a step ahead of his analysands.

The first psychoanalysts who felt compelled to *group* themselves in a *movement* inevitably set their sights on utopian goals. Their aim, similar to that of other utopian movements, religious or political, was to promote self-fulfilment, happiness. Such an aim is impractical. It is difficult enough to define, let alone to attain. Its achievement cannot be scientifically verified and is constantly placed in jeopardy by those who insist on having the last word, and those overly cautious souls who seek refuge in the 'collective wisdom' of majority opinion. The Church is infallible, the Party is always right. In the psychoanalytic movement the leader or the majority is always right. All others are under suspicion of no longer 'being analysts'. Freud was convinced that were Ferenczi to become active again in the International Psychoanalytical Association and be elected its President, he would be 'saved', because he would again be surrounded and influenced by peers who, collectively, were in the right. Despite his unflinching loyalty to Freud, Ernest Jones was aware of the *quasi religious* fervour of what some were beginning to call the psychoanalytical 'movement'. He placed the word 'movement' in quotation marks 'to pillory it, so to speak'. And Jones adds,

> our would-be scientific activities ... partook rather of the nature of a religious movement, and amusing parallels were drawn. Freud was of course the Pope of the new sect, if not a still higher Personage, to whom all owed obeisance; his writings were the sacred text, credence in which was obligatory on the supposed infallibilists who had undergone the necessary conversion, and there were not lacking the heretics who were expelled from the church. It was a pretty obvious caricature to make, but

the minute element of truth in it was made to serve in place of the reality, which was far different.

The picture I saw, on the contrary, was one of active discussion and disagreement that often enough deteriorated into controversy; and, as for 'orthodoxy', it would be easy to find any psycho-analyst who did not hold a different opinion from Freud on some matter or other. Freud himself, it is true, was a man who disliked any form of fighting, and who deprecated so-called scientific controversy on the very good ground that nine-tenths of it is actuated by other motives than the search for truth (Jones, 1959, pp. 205–206).

Early psychoanalytic controversies caused such men as Adler and Jung to break away from the international 'movement'. Later, controversial figures such as Ferenczi and Melanie Klein were able to express dissenting views and still remain members. As the number of analysts grew and spread geographically, *pluralism* came to be an accepted fact. Psychoanalysis dealt with its pluralism the way most utopian societies deal with theirs, that is to say 'ecumenically', while at the same time redefining more forcefully the lines that separate its members from 'outsiders'. In psychoanalysis, certain basic tenets are regarded as important and lend unity to the movement, but within their framework diversity of opinion is considered legitimate.[5] Oaths of loyalty such as Ferenczi's affirmation that he would not become 'a second Stekel' became superfluous (letter from Ferenczi to Freud of 27 December 1931), even though the mechanisms and interpersonal relations characteristic of the two epochs may coexist.

The vicissitudes of the times also helped to determine events within the movement. The authoritarian structure of its early phases was a faithful reflection of the social institutions of the Dual Austro–Hungarian Monarchy and of the 'Successor States'—Austria, Hungary, Czechoslovakia and Yugoslavia as they existed between 1910 and 1930. Emigration—the 'cultural dispersion' of psychoanalysis because of the Nazi persecutions—to English-speaking countries confronted analysts with other traditions and different ways of resolving conflicts. The first official psychoanalytic organization to give formal recognition to more than one school of thought was the British Society. In France and in Italy, professional organizations took more time to become democratic. When the Paris Society was in trouble, Lagache called in Balint and the London Group to ensure fair play; after bitter struggle, several schools and several currents were recognized on an equal footing. The various trends reflect different conceptions of psychoanalysis, different interpretations of its history, which might be called contradictory alternatives. It should be pointed out, however, that psychoanalysts usually do not limit themselves to one point of view, but rather draw on various sources in their practice.

These considerations make it possible to understand more readily how, for Ferenczi and others, technical problems were transformed into questions of loyalty to the movement and to individuals: to Freud, to colleagues and to peers. Under such circumstances, the only ones who were able to arrive at a historical or psychoanalytical understanding of technical problems were members of the fringe group such as Ferenczi and Balint. Although it was a painful process for them, they struggled courageously to overcome taboos. More orthodox members, smug in the knowledge that they were the keepers of 'the truth', were not inclined to strike a blow at it. Only once the taboos had been overcome was it possible to use psychoanalytic knowledge to understand psychoanalysis itself. The attitude of Freud himself was no doubt ambiguous, torn as he was between his aversion for deeply regressed patients and his intuitive sense that regression was an important technical issue. At times he showed keen interest in the topic, at others he overlooked or was reluctant to broach it. In the latter mood, he made statements such as the one found in his correspondence with Edoardo Weiss: 'The ... patient ... is obviously a scoundrel who is not worth your trouble' (Weiss, 1970, p. 36). Or as Ferenczi, in his diary, reported that Freud had told him: 'Patients are nothing but riffraff. The only useful purposes they serve are to help us earn a living and to provide learning material. In any case, we cannot help them' (Ferenczi, 1985, p. 148).

Because Ferenczi and Balint had the courage to ask challenging questions, they, as well as a host of others who succeeded them, were able to approach technical questions without preconceived notions. They were aware that the serious consideration of *practice* is indispensable to the understanding of theory. This basic *preoccupation* with practice is reflected in their respective work. 'Thalassa' (Ferenczi, 1924 [268]) can only be understood in the light of Ferenczi's interest in regression. By the same token, Balint's writings on instincts and drives can only be understood in the light of his efforts to understand the object relationship of drives as it is presented in clinical practice.

It goes without saying that psychoanalysis gains nothing by institutional decrees on scientific matters; but a better understanding of the origins of these controversies and of the inevitable intricacy of psychoanalytic theory and practice would certainly contribute towards clarification.

Even theory presents a number of difficulties. There were many phases in exploring the unconscious mind. Freud's work did not develop in smooth, continuous fashion but in successive leaps as resistances were overcome and new meanings emerged. Because it grew without preconceived aims, its logic is different from that of deductive or experimental science. It was built up in completely unprecedented fashion. Each new discovery opened up new perspectives. Recent acquisitions did not necessarily invalidate or exclude previous observations, nor did all elements necessarily complement each other. The new science did not follow Hegelian principles, by which a thesis and an antithesis would be resolved into a synthesis on a higher level. Freud never gave a definitive synthesis of his work. Each new perspective resulted in a conceptualization that enabled it to be encompassed in the general discussion. Freud never took the matter further. Contrary to popular opinion alluding to the first and second topographical systems, Freud's work does not contain two theories, but rather an unbroken sequence of successive new concepts such as the significance of dreams (1900), drives, and transference, followed by introjection, mourning, the death instinct, etc. His most systematic works, such as his 'Introduction to Psychoanalysis' and his 'New Lectures', are like imaginary presentations allowing for 'open discussion'. Psychoanalysts who explore the field prepared by Sigmund Freud adopt an approach to its problems that is compatible with their own sensitivities and experience, their contact with analysands and with the cultural context of the moment. 'Elective affinities' between analyst and analysand, personality, stage of life, the analyst's environment, will determine the problems that will be dealt with. None of these factors, alone or in combination, renders psychoanalytic theory incoherent. Its coherency resides in its *method* and in the *topics* it explores: the abysses of the human mind.

As new knowledge and meanings emerge, emphasis shifts and interest waxes and wanes, so that representations are far from being crystallized. In so far as psychoanalytic theory is an interpretation of human behaviour explained in various ways, elements are of necessity organized differently by each individual according to his propensities. For some, the Oedipus complex is the main determinant of human behaviour in general, and of love and hate in particular. For others, the quality of relationship with the mother is of prime importance and subsequently determines the ability of the individual to confront the triangular situation. Pre-genital versus genital, father versus mother, object versus narcissismic—around these antithetical concepts the discussions are articulated that clothe the history of psychoanalytic ideas. Since Freud and Ferenczi, the analytic model has oscillated between a myriad alternatives: individual metapsychology or a description of the analytic field in interpersonal or intrapersonal terms; a detached analyst-observer or a participating analyst (and, if participating, to what degree?); analysis as a game or as serious business, a cure, a treatment for sick people; nature or nurture as a determinant of neuroses; drives versus environment; single trauma versus long-term relations, or, in the terminology of geology, 'graduation' in opposition to 'catastrophism'.

The choice of position depends largely on personal experiences, individual temperament, subjective maps of the psychic underworld. Every analyst has his own theory. Some state theirs explicitly by writing and by teaching, while others keep theirs implicit. Moreover, theories are modified according to the interpersonal relations in which the analyst engages. To some extent, they vary with each analysand.

Moreover, such alternatives rarely present themselves as such, but rather as 'complementary' ideas. Indeed, for the majority of analysts today, they are, as it were, 'complemental series'—*Ergänzungen* to Freud (Freud, 1905d, 7:239).

For a minority, on the other hand, they represent alternative ideas that must either be *adhered to* or *rejected*. Accordingly, Ferenczi will be regarded as a new prophet or as a deviant, a heretic—perhaps, the father of all 'deviations'? That depends on how the word 'deviation' is understood. If it expresses a break with the fundamental discoveries of Freud and with his creation of a particular *practice,* the *instrument* of those discoveries, then the answer is an unequivocal no. If, however, 'deviation' is intended to convey experiment, new research and openings towards new horizons, the answer is clearly a yes.

Such openings created by Ferenczi were examined anew and then transmitted by Balint. They include the importance attributed to practice rather than to speculative theory detached from it; the personal involvement of the analyst as creator of, and participant in, the analytic situation; the descriptive rather than the prescriptive examination of the psychoanalytic situation. They are concerned with strengthening the forces of change in treatment and its effectiveness in adapting to an individual's suffering, whatever its depth and gravity. They describe the analytic field in terms of the inter-personal and inter-subjective, viewing the human being as composed of an interactive self. They regard as decisive the influence of the family environment, from the viewpoint of traumata as well as from the early 'maternal environment'. What becomes evident throughout is the constant interplay of a vision of mankind with a psychoanalytic theory that expresses that vision.

Ferenczi's heritage was brought to London by Balint and transmitted to the Independent Group and beyond—in some aspects, for instance, to the Kleinians. It proved itself by the resultant incredible richness in the opening up of the practice of psychoanalysis and its theory as well as its fundamental conceptual orientations. Over and above this important historical axis, it undoubtedly inspired the research on the technique of F. Alexander, the innovations of S. Rado, the interest in children of Margaret Mahler (who considered herself his successor), of René Spitz and others. One might also mention the probable influences of his disciples in America—G. Róheim, I. de Forest, E. Severn, C. Thompson, S. Lorand and others—more difficult to verify.

Reflection raises questions about psychoanalytic controversies. The epistemology of this science is still in its infancy. The naive hope of creating a science 'like any other' has given way to the realization that the 'meta-language' constituted by psychoanalytic theory can only be validated by constant reference to experience, to the practice on which it is founded. Ultimately, psychoanalytic *controversies* address the issue of psychoanalytic *practice*.

NOTES

1. Freud's relations with his pupils, as well as the interpersonal relations among the first generation of analysts, were thoroughly explored by Roazen in a 1975 publication. A 1976 article by F. Roustang deals with the same topic in the light of the correspondence between Freud and Jung, published in 1974.

2. 'In regard to your allegation that ... I misuse psychoanalysis to keep my students in a state of infantile dependency ... I prefer not to judge' (Freud, 1974, p. 537).

3. At the Munich Congress, Jung was re-elected President of the International Psychoanalytical Association by 30 votes against 22 abstentions, despite Freud's disapproval and the recommendations put forward by the Committee. Evidently, the majority did not agree with Freud that Jung's ideas made him an outcast from the psychoanalytic movement.

4. The unconscious we seek to uncover has sought refuge in more remote areas of the individual and collective mind.

5. This was the process that ultimately ushered in the second phase in the history of the analytic movement, which Freud had also foreseen. 'Among half a dozen men of different characters complete agreement on all matters of scientific detail and all questions that break new ground is neither possible nor even desirable. The only condition on which our fertile co-operation depends is that none of us should leave the common ground of psychoanalytic assumptions' (letter, 15 February 1924, in Freud, 1965a, p. 345).

REFERENCES

A bibliography of the works of Michael Balint is given in Appendix B.

The most complete list of the works of Sándor Ferenczi is included in Ferenczi's *Schriften zur Psychoanalyse* (2 vols.), edited by M. Balint (Frankfurt am Main: Fischer, 1970).

A listing of Freud's works can be found in A. Tyson & I. Strachey (1956), 'A chronological hand-list of Freud's work', *International Journal of Psycho-Analysis 37*:18–33.

Assoun, P. L. (1981). *Introduction à l'épistémologie freudienne.* Paris: Payot.

Balint, A. (1936). 'Handhabung der Übertragung auf Grund der Ferenczischen Versuche'. *Internationale Zeitschrift für Psychoanalyse, 22*:47–58.

———— (1939). 'Love for the mother and mother love'. In M. Balint (1965a), *Primary Love and Psycho-analytic Technique* (2nd ed.). London: Tavistock Publications [reprinted London: Maresfield Library, 1985], pp. 91–108. (American edition: New York: Liveright, 1965.)

Balint, E. (1967). 'Training as an impetus to ego development'. *The Psychoanalytic Forum, 2/1*:55–70.

————— (1968). 'Unconscious communications between husband and wife'. In *What Is Psychoanalysis?* edited by W. Joffe. London: Baillière, Tindall & Cassell, pp. 40–51.

————— (1972). 'Fair shares and mutual concern'. *International Journal of Psycho-Analysis, 53*:61–65.

————— (1973). 'Michael Balint: l'élaboration de ses idées sur le remède-médecin'. *Revue de Médecine Psychosomatique, 4*:3–18.

————— & Norell, J. S. (1973). *Six Minutes for the Patient: Interactions in General Practice Consultation.* London: Tavistock Publications.

Balint, M. (1926a). 'Psychoanalyse und klinische Medizin'. *Zeitschrift für klinische Medizin, 103*:628–645.

————— (1926d). 'A pszichotherapiákról a gyakorló orvos számára'. *Therapia, 5*:148–173.

————— (1933e). 'Character analysis and new beginning'. In M. Balint (1965a), *Primary Love and Psycho-analytic Technique* (2nd ed.). London: Tavistock Publications [reprinted London: Maresfield Library, 1985], pp. 151–164. (American edition: New York: Liveright, 1965.)

————— (1935b). 'Critical notes on the theory of the pregenital organizations of the libido'. In M. Balint (1956a), *Problems of Human Pleasure and Behavior: Classic Essays in Humanistic Psychiatry.* New York: Liveright [reprinted London: Maresfield Library, 1987], pp. 37–58.

————— (1935c). 'The final goal of psycho-analytic treatment'. *International Journal of Psycho-Analysis, 17/2*:206–216.

————— (1936a). 'Eros and Aphrodite'. *International Journal of Psycho-Analysis, 19/2*:199–213.

————— (1937b). 'Early developmental stages of the ego: Primary object-love'. *International Journal of Psycho-Analysis, 30/4*:265–273.

————— (1948a). 'On genital love'. *International Journal of Psycho-Analysis, 29/1*:34–40.

————— (1948b). 'On the psycho-analytic training system'. *International Journal of Psycho-Analysis, 29/3*:163–173.

————— (1948c). 'On Szondi's 'Schicksalsanalyse' and 'Triebdiagnostik', *International Journal of Psycho-Analysis, 29/4*:240–249.

————— (1949a). 'Sándor Ferenczi Obiit 1933'. *International Journal of Psycho-Analysis, 30*:215–219.

————— (1950a). 'Changing therapeutical aims and techniques in psycho-analysis'. *International Journal of Psycho-Analysis, 31/* 1–2:117–124.

———— (1950b). 'On the termination of analysis'. *International Journal of Psycho-Analysis, 31/3*:196–199.

———— (1952a). *Primary Love and Psycho-Analytic Technique.* (1st ed.), London: Hogarth Press; and (2nd and enlarged ed.), London: Tavistock Publications, 1952, 1965 [reprinted 1985]. (American edition: New York: Liveright, 1965.)

———— (1952b). 'New beginning and the paranoid and the depressive syndromes'. *International Journal of Psycho-Analysis, 33/2*:214–224.

———— (1952c). 'On love and hate'. *International Journal of Psycho-Analysis, 33/4*:355–362.

———— (1954c). 'Analytic training and training analysis'. *International Journal of Psycho-Analysis, 35/2*:157–162.

———— (1955a). 'Notes on parapsychology and parapsychological healing'. *International Journal of Psycho-Analysis, 36/1*:31–35.

———— (1955b). 'The doctor, his patient and the illness'. *Lancet, 1*:683–688.

———— (1956a). *Problems of Human Pleasure and Behavior: Classic Essays in Humanistic Psychiatry.* New York: Liveright [reprinted London: Maresfield Library, 1987].

———— (1956b). 'Pleasure, object and libido: Some reflexions on Fairbairn's modifications of psychoanalytic theory'. *British Journal of Medicine and Psychology, 29/2*:162–167.

———— (1957a). *The Doctor, His Patient and the Illness.* London: Pitman Medical Publishing Co.

———— (1958c). 'Sándor Ferenczi's last years' (letter to the Editor). *International Journal of Psycho-Analysis, 39/5*:68.

———— (1959a). *Thrills and Regressions.* London: Hogarth Press [reprinted London: Maresfield Library, 1987].

———— (1960c). 'The regressed patient and his analyst'. *Psychiatry: Journal for the Study of Interpersonal Processes 23/3*:231–243.

———— (1960c). 'The regressed patient and his analyst'. *Psychiatry: Journal for the Study of Interpersonal Processes, 23/3*:231–243.

Organization in Geneva, Switzerland.

———— (1962b). 'The theory of parent–infant relationship'. *International Journal of Psycho-Analysis, 43/4–5*:251–252.

_____ (1963b). 'The malignant and the benign forms of regression'. *Bulletin of the Association of Psycho-Analytic Medicine*, 3/2:20–28.

_____ (1964f). 'Preface'. In S. Ferenczi, *Bausteine zur Psychoanalyse, Vol. 1. Theorie* (The Complete Works of Sándor Ferenczi in German, 2nd ed.). Bern: Huber, pp. 7–8.

_____ (1964g). 'Préface'. In *Psychanalyse (Oeuvres complètes) by Sándor Ferenczi, Vol. 1*. Paris: Payot, 1948 and 1982, pp. 7–8.

_____ (1965a). *Primary Love and Psycho-analytic Technique* (2nd and enlarged edition). London: Tavistock Publications [reprinted London: Maresfield Library, 1985]. (1st ed. 1952a.) (American edition: New York: Liveright, 1965.)

_____ (1966b). 'Sándor Ferenczi's technical experiments'. In *Psychoanalytic Techniques*, edited by B. B. Wolman. New York: Basic Books, pp. 147–167.

_____ (1968a). *The Basic Fault: Therapeutic Aspects of Regression*. London: Tavistock Publications.

_____ (1970c). 'La genèse de mes idées'. *Gazette médicale de France*, 77:457–466.

_____ (1970f). 'Préface'. In *Psychanalyse (Oeuvres complètes), by Sándor Ferenczi, Vol. 2*. Paris: Payot, pp. 7–10.

_____ (1985 [1969i]). 'Introduction au Journal de S. Ferenczi'. In S. Ferenczi, *Journal clinique*. Paris: Payot, pp. 13–18.

_____ & Balint, A. (1939). 'On transference and counter-transference'. *International Journal of Psycho-Analysis*, 20/3–4:223–230.

_____ & Balint, E. (1961). *Psychotherapeutic Techniques in Medicine*. London: Tavistock Publications.

_____, Balint, E., Gosling, R., & Hildebrand, P. (1966). *A Study of Doctors*. London: Tavistock Publications.

_____, Ornstein, P., & Balint E. (1972). *Psychotherapy: An Example of Applied Psychoanalysis*. London: Tavistock Publications.

_____ & S. Tarachow (1952). 'General concepts and theory of psycho-analytic therapy'. *Analytical Survey of Psychoanalysis*, 1:227–239.

Bibring, G. (1932). 'Bericht über das therapeutisch-technische Seminar'. *Internationale Zeitschrift für Psychoanalyse*, 18:271–273.

Bion, W. R. (1967). 'Notes on memory and desire'. *Psychoanalytic Forum*, 2:271–280.

Blanton, S. (1971). *Diary of My Analysis with Sigmund Freud*. New York: Hawthorn Books.

Boss, M. (1973). "Medard Boss". In *Psychotherapie in Selbstdarstellungen*, edited by L. Pongratz. Bern: Huber.

Braham, R. L. (1981). *The Politics of Genocide: The Holocaust in Hungary* (2 vols.). New York: Columbia University Press.

Chertok, L., & de Saussure, R. (1973). *Naissance du Psychanalyste*. Paris: Payot.

Cremerius, J. (1983). 'Die Sprache der Zärtlichkeit und der Leidenschaft: Reflexionen zu Sándor Ferenczi's Wiesbadener Vortrag von 1932'. *Psyche, 37*:988–1015.

Dicks, H. V. (1970). *Fifty Years of the Tavistock Clinic*. London: Routledge & Kegan Paul.

Doolittle, H. (1956). *Tribute to Freud*. Boston: David R. Godine.

Dupont, J. (1982). 'Préface'. In *Ferenczi-Groddeck: Correspondence (1921–1933)*. Paris: Payot, pp. 11–37.

————— (1985). 'Avant-propos'. In Ferenczi, S., *Journal clinique*. Paris: Payot, pp. 23–40.

—————, Viliker, M., & Garnier, Ph. (1978). 'Note du traducteur'. In S. Ferenczi, *Psychanalyse, Vol. 2*. Paris: Payot, pp. 11–12.

Eissler, K. (1953). 'The effect of the structure of the ego on psychoanalytic technique'. *Journal of the American Psychoanalytic Association, 1*:104–143.

Eitingon, M. (1933). 'Abschiedsworte an Sándor Ferenczi'. *Imago, 19*:289–295.

Ellenberger, H. (1970). *The Discovery of the Unconscious*. New York: Basic Books.

Farkasházy, M. (1982). 'Rue Mészáros No 12', *Le Coq-Héron, 85*:50–51.

Federn, P. (1933). 'S. Ferenczi'. *Internationale Zeitschrift für Psychoanalyse, 19*:305–321.

Fenichel, O. (1935). 'Zur Theorie der psychoanalytischen Technik'. *Internationale Zeitschrift für Psychoanalyse, 21*:78–95.

————— (1941). *Problems of Psychoanalytic Technique*. Albany, N.Y.: The Psychoanalytic Quarterly.

————— (1980 [1938]). 'Theoretical implications of the didactic analysis'. *Annual of Psychoanalysis, 8*:21–35.

Ferenczi, S. (1909 [67]). 'Introjection and transference'. In *First Contributions to Psycho-Analysis*. London: Hogarth Press, 1955 [reprinted London: Maresfield Library, 1980], pp. 35–93.

————— (1911 [79]). 'On the organization of the psycho-analytical movement'. In *Final Contributions to the Problems and Methods of Psycho-Analysis*. London: Hogarth Press, 1955 [reprinted London: Maresfield Library, 1980], pp. 299–307.

———— (1912 [97]). 'Exploring the unconscious'. In *Final Contributions to the Problems and Methods of Psycho-Analysis*. London: Hogarth Press, 1955 [reprinted London: Maresfield Library, 1980], pp. 308–312.

———— (1913 [104]). 'Taming of a wild horse'. In *Final Contributions to the Problems and Methods of Psycho-Analysis*. London: Hogarth Press, 1955 [reprinted London: Maresfield Library, 1980], pp. 336–340.

———— (1913 [105]). 'To whom does one relate one's dreams? In *Further Contributions to the Theory and Technique of Psycho-Analysis*. London: Hogarth Press, 1955 [reprinted London: Maresfield Library, 1980], p. 349.

———— (1913 [115]). 'A transitory symptom: The position during treatment'. In *Further Contributions to the Theory and Technique of Psycho-Analysis*. London: Hogarth Press, 1955 [reprinted London: Maresfield Library, 1980], p. 242.

———— (1914 [138]). 'Sensations of giddiness at the end of the psycho-analytic session'. In *Further Contributions to the Theory and Technique of Psycho-Analysis*. London: Hogarth Press, 1955 [reprinted London: Maresfield Library, 1980], pp. 239–241.

———— (1914 [139]). 'On falling asleep during the analysis'. In *Further Contributions to the Theory and Technique of Psycho-Analysis*. London: Hogarth Press, 1955, [reprinted London: Maresfield Library, 1980], pp. 249–250.

———— (1919 [210]). 'Technical difficulties in the analysis of a case of hysteria'. In *Further Contributions to the Theory and Technique of Psycho-Analysis*. London: Hogarth Press, 1955 [reprinted London: Maresfield Library, 1980], pp. 189–197.

———— (1919 [216]). 'On the technique of psycho-analysis'. In *Further Contributions to the Theory and Technique of Psycho-Analysis*. London: Hogarth Press, 1955 [reprinted London: Maresfield Library, 1980], pp. 177–189.

———— (1921 [234]). 'The further development of the active therapy in psycho-analysis'. In *Further Contributions to the Theory and Technique of Psycho-Analysis*. London, Hogarth Press, 1955 [reprinted London: Maresfield Library, 1980], pp. 198–217.

———— (1924 [264]) (with O. Rank). *The Development of Psycho-*

Analysis. New York and Washington: Nervous and Mental Disease Publishing Co.

——— (1924 [266]). 'Altató és ébresztö tudomány' [Soothing and arousing science]. *Nyugat*, No. 1.

——— (1924 [267]). 'Ignotus, a megértö' [A comprehending mind]. *Nyugat*, No. 23.

——— (1924 [268]). 'Thalassa: A theory of genitality.' *Psychoanalytic Quarterly*, 1938.

——— (1926 [271]). 'Contra-indications to the "active" psychoanalytical technique'. In *Further Contributions to Theory and Technique of Psycho-Analysis.* London: Hogarth Press, 1955 [reprinted London: Maresfield Library, 1980], pp. 217–230.

——— (1928 [282]). 'The problem of the termination of the analysis'. In *Final Contributions to the Problems and Methods of Psycho-Analysis.* London: Hogarth Press, 1955 [reprinted London: Maresfield Library, 1980], pp. 77–86.

——— (1928 [283]). 'The elasticity of psycho-analytical technique'. In *Final Contributions to the Problems and Methods of Psycho-Analysis.* London: Hogarth Press, 1955 [reprinted London: Maresfield Library, 1980], pp. 87–101.

——— (1928 [306]). 'Über den Lehrgang des Psychoanalytikers'. In *Bausteine zur Psychoanalyse, Band III: Arbeiten aus den Jahren 1908–1933.* Bern: Huber, 1964, pp. 468–489. [Not included in English editions of Ferenczi's works.]

——— (1929 [287]). 'The unwelcome child and his death instinct'. In *Final Contributions to the Problems and Methods of Psycho-Analysis.* London: Hogarth Press, 1955 [reprinted London: Maresfield Library, 1980], pp. 102–107.

——— (1930 [291]). 'The principle of relaxation and neocatharsis'. In *Final Contributions to the Problems and Methods of Psycho-Analysis.* London: Hogarth Press, 1955 [reprinted London: Maresfield Library, 1980], pp. 108–125.

——— (1931 [292]). 'Child analysis in the analysis of adults'. In *Final Contributions to the Problems and Methods of Psycho-Analysis.* London: Hogarth Press, 1955 [reprinted London: Maresfield Library, 1980], pp. 126–142.

——— (1932 [308]). 'Notes and Fragments'. In *Final Contributions to the Problems and Methods of Psycho-Analysis.* London: Hogarth Press, 1955 [reprinted London: Maresfield Library, 1980], pp. 216–279.

_____ (1933 [293]). 'Freud's influence on medicine'. In *Final Contributions to the Problems and Methods of Psycho-Analysis*. London: Hogarth Press, 1955 [reprinted London: Maresfield Library, 1980], pp. 143–155.

_____ (1933 [294]). 'Confusion of tongues between adults and the child'. In *Final Contributions to the Problems and Methods of Psycho-Analysis*. London: Hogarth Press, 1955 [reprinted London: Maresfield Library, 1980], pp. 156–167.

_____ (1936 [297]). *A pszichoanalizis rövid ismertetése*. Budapest: Pantheon Kiadás.

_____ (1968). *Psychanalyse 1*. Paris: Payot.

_____ (1970). *Psychanalyse 2*. Paris: Payot.

_____ (1974). *Psychanalyse 3*. Paris: Payot.

_____ (1982). *Psychanalyse 4*. Paris: Payot.

_____ (1985). *Journal clinique*. Paris: Payot.

_____ & Groddeck, G. (1982). *Correspondance (1921–1933)*. Paris: Payot.

Freud, A. (1936). *The Ego and The Mechanisms of Defence*. London: Hogarth Press, 1937.

Freud, S. (1895a). 'Review of Edinger's "Eine neue Theorie über die Ursachen einiger Nervenkrankheiten, insbesondere der Neuritis und Tabes"'. *Wiener klinische Rundschau, 9/2*:27–28.

_____ (1895d) (with J. Breuer). 'Studies on hysteria'. *Standard Edition, 2*:1–306. London: Hogarth Press, 1955.

_____ (1900a). 'The interpretation of dreams'. *Standard Edition, 4/5*:1–622. London: Hogarth Press, 1953.

_____ (1904a). 'Freud's psycho-analytic procedure'. *Standard Edition, 7*:249–254. London: Hogarth Press, 1953.

_____ (1905d). 'Three essays on the theory of sexuality'. *Standard Edition, 7*:123–243. London: Hogarth Press, 1953.

_____ (1905e). 'Fragment of an analysis of a case of hysteria'. *Standard Edition, 7*:1–122. London: Hogarth Press, 1953.

_____ (1909d). 'Notes upon a case of obsessional neurosis'. *Standard Edition, 10*:155–249. London: Hogarth Press, 1955.

_____ (1910d). 'The future prospects of psycho-analytic therapy'. *Standard Edition, 11*:141–151. London: Hogarth Press, 1957.

_____ (1911e). 'The handling of dream-interpretation in psycho-analysis'. *Standard Edition, 12*:89–96. London: Hogarth Press, 1958.

_____ (1912b). 'The dynamics of transference'. *Standard Edition, 12*:97–108. London: Hogarth Press, 1958.

———— (1912e). 'Recommendations to physicians practising psycho-analysis'. *Standard Edition, 12*:111–120. London: Hogarth Press, 1958.

———— (1913c). 'On beginning the treatment (further recommendations on the technique of psycho-analysis I)'. *Standard Edition, 12*:123–144. London: Hogarth Press, 1958.

———— (1914d). 'On the history of the psycho-analytic movement'. *Standard Edition, 14*:7–66. London: Hogarth Press, 1957.

———— (1914g). 'Remembering, repeating and working-through'. *Standard Edition, 12*:147–156. London: Hogarth Press, 1958.

———— (1916–1917). 'Introductory lectures on psychoanalysis'. *Standard Edition* (Parts I and II), *15*:9–239; (Part III), *16*:243–463. London: Hogarth Press, 1961 and 1963.

———— (1917e). 'Mourning and melancholia'. *Standard Edition, 14*:243–258. London: Hogarth Press, 1957.

———— (1918b). 'From the history of an infantile neurosis'. *Standard Edition, 17*:7–121. London: Hogarth Press, 1955.

———— (1919a [1918]). 'Lines of advance in psycho-analytic therapy'. *Standard Edition, 17*:159–168. London: Hogarth Press, 1955.

———— (1923a). Two encyclopaedia articles ('A: Psycho-analysis; B: The libido theory'). *Standard Edition, 18*:235–259. London: Hogarth Press, 1955.

———— (1923b). 'The ego and the id'. *Standard Edition, 19*:12–66. London: Hogarth Press, 1961.

———— (1925d). 'An autobiographical study'. *Standard Edition, 20*:7–70. London: Hogarth Press, 1959.

———— (1926e). 'The question of lay analysis'. *Standard Edition, 20*:183–250. London: Hogarth Press, 1959.

———— (1930a). 'Civilization and its discontents'. *Standard Edition, 21*:64–145. London: Hogarth Press, 1961.

———— (1932c). 'My contact with Joseph Popper-Lynkeus'. *Standard Edition, 22*:219–224. London: Hogarth Press, 1964.

———— (1933a). 'New introductory lectures on psycho-analysis'. *Standard Edition, 22*:1–182. London: Hogarth Press, 1964.

———— (1933c). 'Sándor Ferenczi'. *Standard Edition, 22*:227–229. London: Hogarth Press, 1964.

———— (1937c). 'Analysis terminable and interminable'. *Standard Edition, 23*:209–254. London: Hogarth Press, 1964.

———— (1940a). 'An outline of psycho-analysis'. *Standard Edition, 23*:139–208. London: Hogarth Press, 1964.

_____ (1960a). *Correspondence (1873–1939)*, edited by E. Freud & L. Freud. New York: Basic Books.

_____ (1963a). *Psychoanalysis and Faith: The Letters of Sigmund Freud and Oskar Pfister*, edited by E. Freud & H. Meng. New York: Basic Books.

_____ (1965a). *A Psycho-Analytic Dialogue: The Letters of Sigmund Freud and Karl Abraham (1907–1926)*, edited by H. Abraham & E. Freud. New York: Basic Books.

_____ (1974). *The Freud/Jung Letters: The Correspondence between Sigmund Freud and C. G. Jung*, edited by W. McGuire. Princeton, N.J.: Princeton University Press.

Fromm, E. (1970). *The Crisis of Psychoanalysis*. London: Jonathan Cape, 1971.

Gedo, J., & Goldberg, A. (1973). *Models of the Mind*. Chicago, Ill.: University of Chicago Press.

Gill, M. (1982). *Analysis of Transference, Vol. I: Theory and Technique*. New York: International Universities Press.

Girard, C. (1983). 'Présence de Sándor Ferenczi: Eléments bibliographiques'. *Revue Française de Psychanalyse, 47/5*:1185–1195.

Glover, E. (1924). '"Active Therapy" and Psycho-Analysis'. *International Journal of Psycho-Analysis, 5*:269–311.

_____ (1931). 'The therapeutic effect of inexact interpretations: A contribution to the theory of suggestion'. *International Journal of Psycho-Analysis, 12/4*:397–411.

_____ (1940). *The Technique of Psycho-Analysis*. New York: International Universities Press, 1955.

Gosling, R. (1966). 'History'. In M. Balint et al., *A Study of Doctors*. London: Tavistock Publications.

Grinker, R. R. (1940). 'Reminiscences of a personal contact with Freud'. In *Freud as We Knew Him*, edited by H. M. Ruitenbeek. Detroit, Mich.: Wayne State University Press.

Grosskurth, Ph. (1986). *Melanie Klein, Her World and Her Work*. New York: Knopf [reprinted London: Maresfield Library, 1985].

Grotjahn, M. (1976). 'Freuds Briefwechsel'. In *Die Psychologie des 20. Jahrhunderts*, edited by D. Eicke. Zurich: Kindler, 1976, pp. 35–146.

Grubrich-Simitis, I. (1986). 'Six letters of Sigmund Freud and Sándor Ferenczi on the interrelationship of psychoanalytic theory and technique.' *International Review of Psycho-Analysis, 13*:259–277.

Grunberger, B. (1974). 'De la technique active à la "confusion de langues"'. *Revue Française de Psychanalyse, 38/4*:521–546.

Haynal, A. (1976). *Depression and Creativity.* New York: International Universities Press, 1985.

Heimann, P. (1950). 'On counter-transference'. *International Journal of Psycho-Analysis, 31*:81–84.

Hermann, I. (1933). 'Zum Triebleben der Primaten'. *Imago, 19*:113–125.

———— (1936). 'Sich-Anklammern—Auf-Suche-Gehen'. *Internationale Zeitschrift für Psychoanalyse, 22*:349–370.

———— (1943). *Instinct filial.* Paris: Denoël, 1972.

———— (1974). 'Souvenirs de Michael Balint (1896–1971)'. *Le Coq-Héron, 85*:45–47.

———— (1975). 'Quelques traits de la personnalité de Sándor Ferenczi'. *Le Coq-Héron, 54*:11–14.

Ignotus, P. (1972). *Hungary.* London: E. Benn.

Jacoby, R. (1983). *The Repression of Psychoanalysis.* New York: Basic Books.

Joffe, W. G. (1971). Manuscript obituary. Balint Archives, Geneva, Switzerland.

Jones, E. (1953). *The Life and Work of Sigmund Freud, Vol. 1.* New York: Basic Books; London: Hogarth Press.

———— (1955). *The Life and Work of Sigmund Freud, Vol. 2.* New York: Basic Books; London: Hogarth Press.

———— (1957). *The Life and Work of Sigmund Freud, Vol. 3.* New York: Basic Books; London: Hogarth Press.

———— (1958). 'Response to M. Balint's "Sándor Ferenczi's last years"' (letter to the Editor). *International Journal of Psycho-Analysis, 39/5*:68.

———— (1959). *Free Associations: Memoirs of a Psychoanalyst.* New York: Basic Books.

Kaiser, H. (1934). 'Probleme der Technik'. *Internationale Zeitschrift für Psychoanalyse, 20*:490–522.

Kanzer, M. (1952). 'The transference neurosis of the Rat Man'. *The Psychoanalytic Quarterly, 21*:181–189.

Karadi, E., & Vezér, E. (eds.) (1980). *A vasárnapi kör. Dokumentumok.* Budapest: Gondolat.

Kardiner, A. (1977). *My Analysis with Freud.* New York: Norton.

Kaufmann, W. (1980). *Discovering the Mind* (3 vols.). New York: McGraw-Hill.

Khan, M. M. R. (1969). 'On the clinical provision of frustrations, recognitions, and failures in the analytic situation.—An essay on Dr. Michael Balint's researches on the theory of psychoanalytic technique. *International Journal of Psycho-Analysis, 50*:237–248.

———— (1973). 'Obituary: Mrs. Alix Strachey (1882–1973). *International Journal of Psycho-Analysis, 54*:370.

Koestler, A. (1952). *An Arrow in the Blue*. New York: The Macmillan Company.

———— (1954). *The Invisible Writing*. Boston, Mass.: Beacon Press.

Kovacs, V. (1931). 'Wiederholungstendenz und Charakterbildung', *Internationale Zeitschrift für Psychoanalyse, 17*:449–463.

———— (1936). 'Training and control-analysis'. *International Journal of Psycho-Analysis, 17*:346–354.

Kris, E. (1951). 'Ego psychology and interpretation in psychoanalytic therapy'. *The Psychoanalytic Quarterly, 20*:15–30.

Lampl-de Groot, J. (1976). 'Personal experience with psychoanalytic technique and theory during the last half century'. *The Psychoanalytic Study of the Child, 31*:283–296.

Lipton, S. (1977). 'The advantages of Freud's technique as shown in his analysis of the Rat Man'. *International Journal of Psycho-Analysis, 58*:255–274.

Lobner, H. (1978). 'Die behandlungstechnischen Diskussionen der Wiener Psychoanalytischen Vereinigung'. *Jahrbuch der Psychoanalyse, X*. Bern: Huber, pp. 169–204.

Lorand, S. (1966). 'Sándor Ferenczi (1873–1933), pioneer of pioneers'. In *Psychoanalytic Pioneers*, edited by F. Alexander, S. Eisenstein & M. Grotjahn. New York: Basic Books.

Lorin, C. (1983). *Le jeune Ferenczi: Premiers écrits 1899–1906*. Paris: Aubier Montaigne.

McDougall, J. (1972). 'L'anti-analysant en analyse: Un portrait clinique et une notion théorique. *Revue Française de Psychanalyse, 36*/2:167–184.

Masson, J. M. (1984). *The Assault on Truth: Freud's Suppression of the Seduction Theory*. New York: Viking [reprinted Harmondsworth, Middlesex: Penguin, 1985].

———— (1985). *The Complete Letters of Sigmund Freud to Wilhelm Fliess 1887–1904*. Cambridge, Mass., and London: The Belknap Press.

Miller, A. (1979). *Das Drama des begabten Kindes und die Suche nach dem wahren Selbst*. Frankfurt am Main: Suhrkamp.

Molnar, M. (1985). *Budapest 1900* (unpublished manuscript).

Money-Kyrle, R. E. (1979). 'Looking backwards—and forwards'. *International Review of Psycho-Analysis, 6*:265–271.

Natterson, J. M. (1966). 'Theodor Reik b. 1888. Masochism in modern man'. In *Psychoanalytic Pioneers*, edited by F. Alexander, S. Eisenstein & M. Grotjahn. New York: Basic Books, pp. 249–264.

Nemes, L. (1985). 'The fate of the Hungarian psychoanalysts during the time of Fascism'. *S. Freud House Bulletin, 9/2*:20–28.

Pontalis, J.-B. (1978). 'Introduction to M. M. R. Khan's "Frustrer, reconnaître et faire défaut dans la situation analytique. A propos des recherches du Dr Balint sur la théorie de la technique psychanalytique"'. *Nouvelle Revue de Psychanalyse, 17*:115.

Racker, H. (1959). *Übertragung und Gegenübertragung*. Munich: Reinhard Verlag.

Rajka, T. (1973). 'Sándor Ferenczi'. *Orvosi Hetilap, 114*:2828–2832.

Reich, W. (1927). 'Zur Technik der Deutung und der Widerstandsanalyse'. *Internationale Zeitschrift für Psychoanalyse, 13*:141–159.

———— (1928). 'Über Charakteranalyse'. *Internationale Zeitschrift für Psychoanalyse, 14/2*:180–196.

———— (1933). *Characteranalysis* (translated by Theodore Wolfe). Rangelay, Maine: Oregone Institute Press, 1945.

Reik, T. (1933). 'New ways in psycho-analytic technique'. *International Journal of Psycho-Analysis, 14*:321–334.

———— (1935). *Surprise and the Psychoanalyst*. New York: Dutton, 1937.

Reverzy-Piguet, C. (1985). *L'enseignement de Ferenczi: Ses préoccupations fondamentales*. Geneva, Switzerland: doctoral thesis, University of Geneva.

Roazen, P. (1975). *Freud and His Followers*. London: Penguin, 1976.

Roustang, F. (1976). *Un destin si funeste*. Paris: Minuit.

Ruitenbeek, H. M. (ed.) (1973). *Freud as We Knew Him*. Detroit, Mich.: Wayne State University Press.

Sabourin, P. (1982). 'Préface'. In S. Ferenczi, *Psychanalyse, Vol. 4*. Paris: Payot, pp. 9–17.

———— (1985). *Ferenczi, Paladin et Grand Vizir secret*. Paris: Editions Universitaires.

Sandler, J. (1976). 'Counter-transference and role-responsiveness'. *International Review of Psycho-Analysis, 3*:43–47.

Saussure, R. de (1956). 'Sigmund Freud'. In *Freud as We Knew Him*, edited by H. M. Ruitenbeck. Detroit. Mich.: Wayne State University Press, 1973, pp. 357–359.

Sterba, R. F. (1934). 'The fate of the ego in analytic therapy'. *International Journal of Psycho-Analysis, 15*:117–126.

―――― (1936). 'Das psychische Trauma und die Handhabung der Übertragung'. *Internationale Zeitschrift für Psychoanalyse, 22*:40–46.

―――― (1982). *Reminiscences of a Viennese Psychoanalyst.* Detroit, Mich.: Wayne State University Press.

Strachey, J. (1934). 'The nature of the therapeutic action of psycho-analysis'. *International Journal of Psycho-Analysis, 15*:127–159.

Sutherland, J. (1971). 'Michael Balint (1896–1970)'. *International Journal of Psycho-Analysis, 52*:331–333.

Sylvam, B. (1984). 'An untoward event, ou la guerre du trauma, de Breuer à Freud, de Jones à Ferenczi'. *Confrontations, 12*:101–122.

Szegö, J. (1964). *Bartók Béla élete.* Bukarest: Ifjusági Könyvkiadó.

Torok, M. (1984). 'La correspondance Ferenczi–Freud: La vie de la lettre dans l'histoire de la psychanalyse'. *Confrontations, 12*:119–122.

Weiss, E. (1970). *Sigmund Freud as a Consultant.* New York: Intercontinental Medical Book Corporation.

Will, H. (1985). 'Freud, Groddeck und die Geschichte des "Es"'. *Psyche, 39*:150–169.

Winnicott, D. W. (1947). 'Through paediatrics to psycho-analysis'. In *Collected Papers.* London: Tavistock Publications, 1958.

Zetzel, E. R. (1966). '1965: Additional notes upon a case of obsessional neurosis, Freud 1909'. *International Journal of Psycho-Analysis, 47*:123–129.

APPENDICES

Congresses
of the International
Psychoanalytical Association

1st Congress	1908	Salzburg, Austria
2nd Congress	1910	Nuremberg, Germany
3rd Congress	1911	Weimar, Germany
4th Congress	1913	Munich, Germany

1914–1918: World War I

5th Congress	1918	Budapest, Hungary
6th Congress	1920	The Hague, Holland
7th Congress	1922	Berlin, Germany
8th Congress	1924	Salzburg, Austria
9th Congress	1925	Bad Homburg, Germany
10th Congress	1927	Innsbruck, Austria
11th Congress	1929	Oxford, England
12th Congress	1932	Wiesbaden, Germany
13th Congress	1934	Lucerne, Switzerland
14th Congress	1936	Marienbad, Czechoslovakia
15th Congress	1938	Paris, France

1939–1945: World War II

16th Congress	1949	Zurich, Switzerland
17th Congress	1951	Amsterdam, Holland
18th Congress	1953	London, England

19th Congress	1955	Geneva, Switzerland
20th Congress	1957	Paris, France
21st Congress	1959	Copenhagen, Denmark
22nd Congress	1961	Edinburgh, Scotland
23rd Congress	1963	Stockholm, Sweden
24th Congress	1965	Amsterdam, Holland
25th Congress	1967	Copenhagen, Denmark
26th Congress	1969	Rome, Italy
27th Congress	1971	Vienna, Austria
28th Congress	1973	Paris, France
29th Congress	1975	London, England
30th Congress	1977	Jerusalem, Israel
31st Congress	1979	New York, U.S.A.
32nd Congress	1981	Helsinki, Finland
33rd Congress	1983	Madrid, Spain
34th Congress	1985	Hamburg, Germany
35th Congress	1987	Montreal, Canada

Bibliography
of the works of Michael Balint

Marie-Christine Beck

The present list is arranged chronologically. Each publication is identified by the year of publication and a lower-case letter.

As Michael Balint wrote in three languages (Hungarian, German and English) and his writings were widely translated, it is sometimes difficult to distinguish between the original and the translations. We have made every possible effort to clear up ambiguities of this sort.

Translations are listed alongside the original publications to be found under the year in which the original was printed. For ease of cross-reference, the various languages are indicated by number.

We have maintained the spelling of the original titles.

We have used every available source. Most valuable among them was the bibliography in E. Falzeder's doctoral thesis (Salzburg, 1984) and we would like to acknowledge the important bibliographic work accomplished by that author.

1924a. [1923] (with M. Petow). 'Eine jodometrische Bestimmung des Natriums'. *Biochem. Z. 145/3–4*: 242–243.

1924b. 'Eine jodometrische Mikrobestimmung des Natriums'. Berlin, Inaugural thesis [shortened version in *Biochem. Z.*, *150/5–6*: 424–443].

1924c. 'Ein Beweis der Konstanz der [H'] der lebenden Bakterienzelle'. *Biochem. Z.*, *152/1–2*: 92–93.

1924d. (with P. Ruszezynski). 'Eine Mikromethode zur Bestimmung von organischen Substanzen'. *Biochem. Z. 152/3–4*: 246–249.

1925a. (1) 'Wasserstoffionenkonzentration und "Elektropie"', I. *Biochem. Z.*, *165/4–6*: 465–472.

(2) In Hungarian: 'Hydrogenion-concentratio és "elektropia"', I. *Gyógyászat, 66/4*: 82–86, 1926.

1925b. (1) 'Perversio vagy hysteriás tünet?' [Perversion or hysterical symptom?]. Paper given at the Psychoanalytical Society of Berlin, 1923. *Gyólgyászat, 65/49*: 1104–1105.

(2) In English: 'Perversion or a hysterical symptom?' In 1956a(1), pp. 182–187.

1925c. Book review: *Zur Periodenlehre*, by W. Fliess. *Int. Z. Psa.*, *11*: 491.

1925d. Book review: *Warum wir sterben?* by A. Liepschütz. *Int. Z. Psa.*, *11*: 491.

1925e. Book review: *Der Ursprung des Lebens*, by R. Stó4lzle. *Int. Z. Psa.*, *11*: 491.

1926a. (1) 'Psychoanalyse und klinische Medizin'. *Z. Klin. Med.*, *103/5–6*: 628–645.

(2) In Hungarian: 'Psychoanalysis és belgyógyászat'. *Gyógyászat, 66/19*: 439–445.

1926b. 'Hydrogenion-concentratió és "elektropia"' [Concentration of the hydrogen ions and "electropia"] II. *Gyógyászat, 66/26*: 611–613.

1926c. 'Gepuffertes Wasser für die Romanowsky-Giemsa-Färbung'. *Klin. Wschr. 5/4*: 147–148.

1926d. 'A pszichotherapiáról a gyakorló orvos számára' [On psychotherapies by the general practitioner]. *Terapia* (Budapest), *5*: 148–173 [reprinted in *Terapia* (Bratislava), *6/22*: 1–5, 1927].

1926e. Book review: *Testi tünetek psychogenesise és pszichotherapiája* [Psychotherapy and psychogenesis of the somatic symptoms], by O. Schwarz. *Gyógyászat, 66/13*: 310–311.

1927a. (1) Book review: *Die hó4chste Nerventätigkeit (das Verhalten) von Tieren. Eine zwanzigjährige Prüfung der objektiven Forschung. Bedingte Reflexe*, by I. P. Pavlov (German title, Hungarian text with German quotations). *Gyógyászat, 67/43*: 964–970.
   (2) In English: I. P. Pavlov, in 1956a(1), pp. 223–234.

1928a. 'Ueber die Todesangst. Ein kasuistischer Beitrag'. Paper given on 19 November 1927 at the Hungarian Psychoanalytical Society. Abstract in: *Int. Z. Psa., 14/2*: 289.

1930a. 'Az orvosi praxis válsága' [The crisis of the medical practice]. *Gyógyászat, 70/19*: 373–375.

1931a. [1929] 'Diskussionen zur Kritik der Libidometrie nach Bernfeld und Feitelberg' (with P. Csillag). Paper given on 31 May 1929 at the Hungarian Psychoanalytical Society. *Imago, 17/3*: 410–413 (resp. 410–420, answer by S. Bernfeld and S. Feitelberg included).

1932a. (1) [1930] 'Psychosexuelle Parallelen zum bioenergetischen Grundgesetz'. *Imago, 18/1*: 14–41 [reprinted in 1965a(3), pp. 13–44].
   (2) In Hungarian: unpublished paper given at the Hungarian Psychoanalytical Society in 1933.
   (3) In French: 'Parallèles psychosexuels de la loi biogénétique fondamentale', in 1965a(4), pp. 13–42.
   (4) In English: 'Psychosexual parallels to the fundamental law of biogenetics', in 1952a(1), and 1965a(1), pp. 3–30.

1933a (1) 'Az érzelemátvitelró4l' [On the transference of emotions]. Paper given at the Hungarian Psychoanalytical Society, 1933. *Gyógyászat, 73/12–13*: 2–12.

(2) In French: 'Le transfert des émotions', in 1965a(4), pp. 190–203.

(3) In English: 'On transference of emotions', in 1965a(1), pp. 165–177. (N.B.: British examples instead of the Hungarian ones).

(4) In German: 'Zur Uebertragung von Affekten', in 1965a(3), pp. 203–218.

1933b. (1) 'Az öregedés lelki problémái'. [Psychical problems of the old age]. Paper given at the Medical Society of Budapest, 1933. *Gyógyászat, 73/33*: 505–509.

(2) In English: 'The psychological problems of growing old', in 1956a(1), pp. 69–85.

1933c (1) 'Zwei Notizen über die erotische Komponente der Ich-Triebe.' *Int. Z. Psa., 19/3*: 428–433 [reprinted in 1965a(3), pp. 45–51].

(2) In French: 'Deux remarques concernant la composante érotique des instincts du Moi', in 1965a(4), pp. 43–49.

(3) In English: 'Two notes on the erotic component of the ego-instincts', in 1965a(1), pp. 31–36.

1933d. 'Ueber die Psychoanalyse des Charakters'. Paper given on 2 February 1933 at the Hungarian Psychoanalytic Society. Abstract in: *Int. Z. Psa., 19/3*: 449.

1933e. (1) 'A jellemanalizis és az újrakezdés' [Character analysis and new beginning]; paper given on 24 June 1932 at the Hungarian Psychoanalytic Society, with an introduction by S. Freud. *Lélekelemzési tanulmányok,* Budapest: Béla Somló, publisher, 1933, pp. 65–79.

(2) In German: 'Charakteranalyse und Neubeginn'. *Int. Z. Psa, 20/1*: 54–65, 1934 [reprinted in 1965a(3), pp. 187–202].

(3) In French: 'Analyse de caractère et renouveau', in 1965a(4), pp. 175–189.

(4) In English: 'Character analysis and new beginning', in 1952a(1), pp. 159–173, and 1965a(1), pp. 151–164 [reprinted London: Maresfield Library, 1985].

1933f. Book review: *Die Krise der Medizin. Lehrbuch der Konstitutionstherapie*, by B. Aschner. *Int. Z. Psa., 19*/3: 452–453.

1934a (1) 'Der Onanieabgewöhnungskampf in der Pubertät'.*Z. Psychoanal. Pädagogik, 8*/11–12: 374–391.

(2) In English: 'The adolescent's fight against masturbation', in 1956a(1), pp. 49–68.

1934b. (1) 'Dr Sándor Ferenczi as a psycho-analyst'. Necrology of 3 October 1933, at the Hungarian Psychoanalytic Society. *Indian J. Psychol., 9*: 19–27 [reprinted in 1956a(1), pp. 235–242].

(2) In Hungarian: 'Ferenczi Sándor mint orvos'. *Gyógyászat, 74*/20: 312–315.

(3) In German: 'Dr. Sándor Ferenczi als Arzt' (typewritten manuscript, Balint Archives, Geneva).

1935a. (1) 'A contribution on Fetishism'. Paper given on 7 December 1934 at the Hungarian Psychoanalytic Society. *Int. J. Psycho-Anal., 16*/4: 481–483 [reprinted in 1956a(1), pp. 171–173].

(2) In German: 'Ein Beitrag zum Fetischismus'. *Int. Z. Psa, 23*/3: 413–414, 1937.

1935b. (1) 'Zur Kritik der Lehre von den prägenitalen Organisationen der Libido'. Paper given on 27 April 1934 at the Hungarian Psychoanalytic Society, with the title 'Prägenital und extragenital', and on 15 May 1935 at the Vienna Psychoanalytic Society. *Int. Z. Psa., 21*: 525–543 [reprinted in 1965a(3), pp. 52–76].

(2) In French: 'Remarques critiques concernant la théorie des organisations prégénitales de la libido', in 1965a(4), pp. 50–73.

(3) In English: 'Critical notes on the theory of the pregenital organizations of the libido', in 1956a(1), pp. 37–58 [reprinted London: Maresfield Library, 1987].

1935c (1) 'Das Endziel der psychoanalytischen Behandlung'. Paper given on 31 August 1934 at the International Congress of Psychoanalysis in Lucerne. *Int. Z. Psa, 21*/1: 36–45 [reprinted in 1965a(3), pp. 219–231].

(2)   In English: 'The final goal of psycho-analytic treatment'. *Int. J. Psycho-Anal.*, *17*/2: 206–216 [reprinted in 1965a(1), pp. 178–188].

(3)   In French: 'Le but final du traitement psychanalytique', in 1965a(4), pp. 204–215.

1936a   (1)   'Eros und Aphrodite'. Paper given on 23 May 1936 at the Hungarian Psychoanalytic Society, and on 7 August 1936 at the 14th International Psychoanalytic Congress in Marienbad. *Int. Z. Psa*, *22*/4: 453–465 [reprinted in 1965a(3), pp. 77–92].

(2)   In English: 'Eros and Aphrodite'. *Int. J. Psycho-Anal.*, *19*/2: 199–213 [reprinted in 1952a(1), and 1965a(1), pp. 59–73].

(3)   In French: 'Eros et Aphrodite', in 1965a(4), pp. 74–90.

1936b   'Ferenczi Sándor', in *Uj lexikon: A tudás és a gyakorlati élet egyetemes enciklopédiája 6 kötetben, Vol. III*. Dante-Pantheon, Budapest, p. 1229, 1937–1938.

1937a.   'A contribution to the psychology of menstruation'. Paper given on 17 November 1933 at the Hungarian Psychoanalytic Society. *Psychoanal. Quart.*, *6*: 346–352 (shortened version) [enlarged version in 1956a(1), pp 174–181].

1937b.   (1)   'Frühe Entwicklungsstadien des Ichs: primäre Objektliebe'. Paper given at the 2nd Vierländertagung in Budapest, 15–17 May 1937. *Imago, 23*: 270–288 [reprinted in 1965a(3), pp. 93–115].

(2)   In English: 'Early developmental stages of the ego: primary object-love'. *Int. J. Psycho-Anal.*, *30*/4: 265–273, 1939 [reprinted in 1952a(1); and 1965a(1), pp. 74–90].

(3)   In French: 'Les premiers stades de développement du Moi. Amour d'object primaire', in 1965a(4), pp. 91–109.

1938a.   'Ferenczi Sándor', in *Uj idök lexikona, Vol. IX–X*, Budapest: Singer és Wolfner, p. 2412.

1939a.   (1)   (with Alice Balint). 'On transference and counter-transference'. *Int. J. Psycho-Anal., 20/*3–4: 223–230 [reprinted in 1952a(1), and 1965a(1), pp. 201–208].

(2)   In French: 'Transfert et contre-transfert', in 1965a(4), pp. 229–236.

(3)   In German: 'Uebertragung und Gegenübertragung', in 1965a(3), pp. 246–254.

1939b.   'Ich-Stärke, Ich-Pädagogik und "Lernen"'. Paper given on 4 November 1938 at the Hungarian Psychoanalytic Society, and at the 15th International Congress of Psychoanalysis, Paris, 1938. *Int. Z. Psa., 24/*4: 417–427 [reprinted in 1965a(3), pp. 232–245. See also 1971c].

(2)   In English: 'Ego strength and education'. *Psychoanal. Quart. 11/*1: 87–95, 1942 [reprinted in 1965a(1), pp. 189–200].

(3)   In French: 'Force du Moi, éducation du Moi et "apprentissage"', in 1965a(4), pp. 216–228.

1941a.   Book Review: *Race, Sex and Environment,* by J. R. de la Marett. *Brit. J. Med. Psychol., 18*: 273, 1939–41.

1942a.   'Reality testing during schizophrenic hallucinations'. *Brit. J. Med. Psychol., 19/*2: 201–214 [reprinted in 1956a(1), pp. 153–170 with the title 'Contributions to reality testing'].

1945a.   'Individual differences of behaviour in early infancy'. Manchester, Medical Sciences, thesis. Shortened version in: *J. Genet. Psychol., 73*: 57–79 and 81–117, 1948 [reprinted in 1956a(1), pp. 125–149].

1948a.   (1)   'On genital love'. Paper given on 26 May 1947 at the Conference of European Psychoanalysts in Amsterdam. *Int. J. Psycho-Anal., 29/*1: 34–40 [reprinted in 1952a(1), and 1965a(1), pp. 109–120].

(2)   In French: 'L'amour génital', in 1965a(4), pp. 129–142.

(3)   In German: 'Ueber genitale Liebe', in 1965a(3), pp. 136–150.

1948b. (1) 'On the psycho-analytic training system'. Com-
             munication of 5 November 1947 at the British
             Psychoanalytic Society. *Int. J. Psycho-Anal., 29*/3:
             163–173 [reprinted in 1965a(1), pp. 253–274].
        (2) In French: 'A propos du système de formation
             psychanalytique', in 1965a(4), pp. 285–308.
        (3) In German: 'Ueber das psychoanalytische Ausbil-
             dungssystem', in 1965a(3), pp. 307–332.

1948c. 'On Szondi's "Schicksalsanalyse" and "Triebdiagnostik"'
        (A review). *Int. J. Psycho-Anal., 29*/4: 240–249 [reprinted
        in 1956a(1), pp. 261–280].

1949a. 'Dr Sándor Ferenczi, obiit 1933'. Introduction to the
        "Ferenczi" number, based upon the paper given on 5 May
        1948 at the British Psychoanalytic Society for the 15th
        anniversary of Ferenczi's death. *Int. J. Psycho-Anal.,
        30*/4: 215–219 [reprinted in 1956a(1), pp. 243–250].

1950a. (1) 'Changing therapeutical aims and techniques in
             psychoanalysis'. Paper given on 2 March 1949 at the
             British Psychoanalytic Society, and in August 1949
             at the 16th International Psychoanalytic Congress
             in Zurich. *Int. J. Psycho-Anal., 31*/1–2: 117–124
             [reprinted in *The Yearbook of Psychoanalysis, 7*:
             175–188, 1951, and in 1965a(1), pp. 209–222].
        (2) In French: 'L'évolution des buts et des techniques
             thérapeutiques en psychanalyse', in 1965a(4), pp.
             237–251.
        (3) In German: 'Wandlungen der therapeutischen Ziele
             und Techniken in der Psychoanalyse', in 1965a(3),
             pp. 255–271.

1950b. (1) 'On the termination of analysis'. Paper given on 2
             March 1949 at the British Psychoanalytic Society.
             Int. J. Psycho-Anal., 31/3: 196–199 [reprinted in
             1952a(1), and 1965a(1), pp. 223–229].
        (2) In French: 'La fin d'analyse', in 1965a(4), pp.
             252–259.
        (3) In German: 'Ueber die Beendigung der Psycho-
             analyse', in 1965a(3), pp. 272–279.
        (4) In Spanish: *Rev. Uruguaya,* 1962/63.

1951a. (1)   'The problem of discipline' (shortened version). *The New Era, 32*: 104–110 [enlarged version in 1956a(1), pp. 34–48].

    (2)   In French: 'Le problème de la discipline'. *Rev. Franç. Psychanal., 15/4*: 463–477.

    (3)   In German: 'Das Problem der Disziplin' (translation of the enlarged version), in *Der psychoanalytische Beitrag zur Erziehungswissenschaft*, by P. Fürstenau (ed.). Darmstadt: Wissenschaftliche Buchgesellschaft, 1974, pp. 165–182.

1951b. 'On punishing offenders', in *Psychoanalysis and Culture. Essays in Honour of Géza Róheim*, by G. B. Wilbur and W. Muensterberger (eds.). New York: International Universities Press, pp. 254–280 [reprinted in 1956a(1), pp. 86–116].

1951c. Book review: *Exploring the unconscious* and *The Book of the Id*, by G. Groddeck. *Int. J. Psycho-Anal., 32*: 250.

1951d. Book review: *Tensions Affecting Understanding*, by D. Klineberg and H. Cantril (eds.). *Int. J. Psycho-Anal., 32*: 251.

1951e. Book review: *The Inner Experience of a Psycho-Analyst*, by Th. Reik. *Int. J. Psycho-Anal., 32*: 326.

1952a. (1)   *Primary Love and Psycho-analytic Technique*. London: Hogarth Press, International Psychoanalytic Library.

    (2)   American edition: New York: Liveright Publishing.

    (3)   See also 1965a(1).

1952b. (1)   'New beginning and the paranoid and the depressive syndromes'. *Int. J. Psycho-Anal., 33/2*: 214–224 [reprinted in 1952a(1), and 1965a(1), pp. 230–249].

    (2)   In French: 'Le renouveau et les syndromes paranoïde et dépressif', in 1965a(4), pp. 260–281.

    (3)   In German: 'Der Neubeginn, das paranoide und das depressive Syndrom', in 1965a(3), pp. 280–303.

1952c. (1)   'On love and hate'. Paper given at the 17th International Congress of Psychoanalysis in Amsterdam in 1951. *Int. J. Psycho-Anal., 33/4*: 355–362 [reprinted in 1952a(1), and 1965a(1), pp. 121–135].

(2) In German: 'Ueber Liebe und Hass'. *Psyche, 6/1*: 19–33, 1952/53 [reprinted in 1965a(3), pp. 151–169].

(3) In French: 'L'amour et la haine', in 1965a(4), pp. 143–159.

1952d. 'Notes on the dissolution of object-representation in modern art'. *J. Aesthetics and Art Crit., 10/4*: 323–327 [reprinted in 1956a(1), pp. 117–124].

1952e. [1950] (with S. Tarachow). 'General concepts and theory of psycho-analytic therapy'. *Ann. Surv. Psychoanal., 1*: 227–240.

1952f. Book review: *Group Life*, by M. I. Greco. *Int. J. Psycho-Anal., 33/1*: 63.

1952g. Book review: *Soviet Psychiatry*, by J. Wortis. *Int. J. Psycho-Anal., 33/1*: 63–64.

1952h. Book review: *Neurosis and Human Growth*, by K. Horney. *Brit. J. Med. Psychol., 25*: 166.

1953a. (1) Editing and preface of *The Psychoanalysis of the Nursery* by Alice Balint. London: Routledge & Kegan Paul (translation of *A gyermekszoba pszicho-logiája*, probably by herself).

(2) American edition: *The Early Years of Life*. New York: Basic Books, 1954.

(3) In German: Preface to *Psychoanalyse der frühen Lebensjahre*. Munich/Basel: Reinhardt, 1966, pp. 7–8.

(4) This book was published also in Hungarian (1931), in German (1932), in French (1937), in Spanish (1939).
See also 1966g.

1954a. 'Method and technique in the teaching of medical psychology. II. Training general practitioners in psycho-therapy'. *Brit. J. Med. Psychol., 27/1–2*: 37–41.

1954b. (1) 'Training general practitioners in psychotherapy'. *Brit. Med. J., 1*: 115–131.

(2) Shortened version: *Brit. J. Med. Psychol., 27/1–2*: 37–41.

(3) In German: 'Psychotherapeutische Ausbildung des

praktischen Arztes'. *Psyche,* 9/6: 370–389, 1955 (translated from the English by M. v. Niederhöffer).

(4)   In French: 'Formation des omnipracticiens à la psychothérapie'. *Psychanalyse,* 2: 221–242, 1956 (translated from the English by D. Lagache).

1954c. (1)   'Analytic training and training analysis'. Paper given on 28 July 1953 at the 18th International Congress of Psychoanalysis in London. *Int. J. Psycho-Anal.,* 35/2: 157–162 [reprinted in 1965a(1), pp. 275–285].

(2)   In German: 'Analytische Ausbildung und Lehranalyse'. *Psyche,* 7/11: 689–699, 1953/54 [reprinted in 1965a(3), pp. 333–346].

(3)   In French: 'Formation analytique et analyse didactique', in 1965a(4), pp. 309–321.

1954d. 'Géza Róheim: An obituary'. *Int. J. Psycho-Anal.,* 35/4: 434–436 [reprinted in 1956a(1), pp. 256–260 with the title 'Géza Róheim, 1891–1953'].

1954e. Book review: *The Life and Ideas of the Marquis de Sade,* by G. Gover. *Int. J. Psycho-Anal.,* 35/1: 78–83 [reprinted in 1956a(1), pp. 251–255].

1955a. 'Notes on parapsychology and parapsychological healing'. *Int. J. Psycho-Anal.,* 36/1: 31–35 [reprinted in 1956a(1), pp. 188–197].

1955b. (1)   'The doctor, his patient and the illness'. Paper given on 26 January 1955 at the Medical Division of the British Society of Psychology. *Lancet*: 683–688, 2 April 1955 [reprinted in 1956a(1), pp. 198–220].

(2)   Also in *Samiksa* (Indian Psychoanalytical Society), 9/3: 173–195.

(3)   Abstract in *B.P.S. Bulletin* No. 26, May 1955, pp. 54–59.

(4)   In Portugese: *O medico, o doente e o doenca,* 1960.

1955c. 'Friendly expanses—horrid empty spaces'. Paper given on 20 October 1954 at the British Psychoanalytic Society. *Int. J. Psycho-Anal.,* 36/4–5: 225–241.

1955d. (with Enid Balint). 'Dynamics of training in groups for psychotherapy'. *Brit. J. Med. Psychol.,* 28/2–3: 135–142.

1955e. (1)   Editing of *Final Contributions to the Problems and Methods of Psychoanalysis*, by S. Ferenczi. London: Hogarth Press, International Psychoanalytical Library.

(2)   American edition: New York: Basic Books.

1955f.   Book review: *Five Copybooks*, by M. Bonaparte. *Int. J. Psycho-Anal.*, *36*/6: 412–414.

1956a. (1)   'Problems of human pleasure and behavior. Classic essays in humanistic psychiatry'. New York: Liveright, 1956.

(2)   English edition: London: Hogarth Press, 1957 [reprinted London: Maresfield Library, 1987].

(3)   Paperback edition: New York: Liveright, 1973.

1956b. (1)   'Pleasure, object and libido: some reflexions on Fairbairn's modifications of psychoanalytic theory'. *Brit. J. Med. Psychol.*, *29*/2: 162–167 [published also in 1956a(1), pp. 281–291].

(2)   Also in *Brit. J. Med.* Brighton: B.M.A., Vol. 29, part 2, pp. 162–167.

(3)   In German: 'Lust, Objekt und Libido. Einige Ueberlegungen zu Fairbairns Modifikationen der psychoanalytischen Theorie' (translated from the English by M. C. Beck). *Z. für psychoanalytische Theorie und Praxis*, Amsterdam: Assen (in press).

1956c. (1)   'Perversions and genitality', in *Perversions, Psychodynamics and Psychotherapy*. New York: Random House, pp. 16–27 [reprinted in 1965a(1), pp. 136–144].

(2)   In French: 'Perversions et génitalité', in 1965a(4), pp. 160–169.

(3)   In German: 'Perversionen und Genitalität'. *Psyche*, *20*/7: 520–528, 1966 [published also in 1965a(3), pp. 170–180].

1956d.   'Domiciliary consultation in psychiatric practice' (letter). *Lancet, 2*: 1389.

1956e.   Editing of *Perversions. Psychodynamics and Therapy* (with Sándor Lorand). New York: Random House, Gramercy Books.

1957a. (1) *The Doctor, his Patient and the Illness.* London: Pitman Medical Publishing [see also 1964a].

(2) American edition: New York: International Universities Press [reprinted in 1964].

(3) In German: *Der Arzt, sein Patient und die Krankheit.* Stuttgart: Klett-Cotta (translated from the English by K. Hügel).

(4) In French: *Le médicin, son malade et la maladie.* Paris: Presses Universitaires de France, 1960 (translated from the English by J. P. Valabrega).

(5) In Hungarian: *Az orvos, a betege és a betegség.* Budapest: Akadémiai Kiadó, 1961.

(6) In Italian: *Il medico, il paziente e la malattia.* Milan: Feltrinelli, 1961 (translated from the English by C. Ranchetti).

(7) In Spanish: *El Médico, el paciente y la enfermedad.* Buenos Aires: Libros Basicos, 1961 (translated from the English by A. Leal).

(8) In Japanese: Tokyo: Y. Ikemi, 1967.

(9) In Swedish: 'Läkaren, patienten och sjukdomen'. Stockholm: Natur och Kultur, 1972 (translated from the English by Ph. Wiking).

1957b. (1) [1956] 'Psychotherapy and the general practitioner', I (Annual Meeting Address).

(2) Shortened version in *Brit. Med. J., 1*/5011: 156–158.

(3) In German: see 1957c.

1957c. Contribution to 'Freud in der Gegenwart', in *Frankfurter Beiträge zur Soziologie, Vol. 6,* Frankfurt/Main: Europäische Verlagsanstalt. [Contains: 'Psychotherapie durch den praktischen Arzt', pp. 87–126, German translation of two chapters of 'The doctor, his patient and the illness', in 1965a(3), pp. 172–191 and 192–212, and 'Sexualität und Gesellschaft', pp. 127–149. Address at the Universities of Heidelberg and Frankfurt during the Freud's centenary celebrations in May 1956. In English: 'Sex and society', in 1956a(1), pp. 11–33.]

1957d. (1) 'Training medical students in psychotherapy'. Paper given to the doctors of the Medical Psychological Division of the University College Hospital, London, October 1957. *Lancet:* 1015–1018, 23 November 1957.

     (2)   In German: 'Die psychotherapeutische Ausbildung der Medizinstudenten'. *Psyche, 12/1*: 73–80, 1958 (translated from the English by K. Hügel).

1957e. 'Criticism of Fairbairn's generalisation about object-relation'. *Brit. J. Philos. Sci.*, 7/28: 323–324.

1957f. (1)   'Die drei seelischen Bereiche'. *Psyche, 11/6*: 321–344 [reprinted in 1968a(3), pp. 11–42].

     (2)   In English: 'The three areas of the mind: Theoretical considerations'. *Int. J. Psycho-Anal., 39/5*: 328–340, 1958 [reprinted in 1968a(1), pp. 3–31, with the title: Part I 'The three areas of the mind'].

     (3)   In French: 'Les trois niveaux de l'appareil psychique'. *Psychanalyse, 6*: 283–312, 1961 [reprinted in 1968a(4), pp. 9–46, with the title: 'Les trois zones de l'apareil psychique', translated from the English by V. N. Smirnoff].

1958a. 'The concepts of subject and object in psychoanalysis'. *Brit. J. Med. Psychol., 31*: 83–91.

1958b. (1)   '"Eröffnungszüge" in der Psychotherapie'. *Dtsch. Med. Wschr., 83/48*: 2117–2122.

     (2)   In English: 'Opening moves in psychotherapy'. *J. Hillside Hosp., 8/1–2*: 9–20, 1959.

1958c. (1)   'Sándor Ferenczi's last years' (letter to the Editor). *Int. J. Psycho-Anal., 39/5*: 68 (commented by E. Jones). Also in *Int. J. Psycho-Anal., 49/1*: 99, 1968.

     (2)   In French: 'Lettre à l'éditeur: Les dernières années de Sándor Ferenczi' in M. Torok (1984 [1983]), 'La correspondance Freud-Ferenczi. La vie de la lettre dans l'histoire de la psychanalyse'. *Confrontations, 12*: 117–118, 1984.

1959a. (1)   'Thrills and Regressions' (with a study by Enid Balint). London: Hogarth Press [reprinted London: Maresfield Library].

     (2)   American edition: New York: International Universities Press.

     (3)   In German: *Angstlust und Regression. Beitrag zur psychologischen Typenlehre*. Stuttgart: Klett, 1960 (translated from the English by K. Wolff with the collaboration of A. Mitscherlich & M. Balint).

(4)   In French: *Les voies de la régression*. Paris: Payot, 1972 (translated from the English by M. Viliker & J. Dupont).

1959b. (1)   'La responsabilité du médecin'. Paper given on 1 July 1959 to The Thames Valley Faculty of the College of General Practitioners. Abstract, *Rev. Méd. Psychosom. 1*/1: 1–12 [reprinted in 1961a(1), pp. 127–139].

(2)   In English: 'The doctor's responsibility'. *Med. World 92*/6: 529–540 [reprinted in 1961a(1), pp. 104–115].

(3)   In German: 'Die Verantwortung des Arztes'. *Psyche, 13*/10: 561–573, 1960 [reprinted in 1961a(3), pp. 140–154].

1960a. 'The marital problem clinic: A problem child of the F.P.A'. *Family Planning, 9*/1: 18–20.

1960b. (1)   'Primary narcissism and primary love'. *Psychoanal. Quart., 29*/1: 6–43 [reprinted in 1968a(1), pp. 34–76].

(2)   In German: 'Primärer Narzissmus und primäre Liebe', in *Jahrbuch der Psychoanalyse, Vol. 1*, pp. 3–34 [reprinted in 1968a(3), pp. 44–93].

(3)   In French: 'Narcissisme primaire et amour primaire', in 1968a(4), pp. 47–105.

1960c. (1)   'The regressed patient and his analyst' (Third Conference In Memoriam Frieda Fromm-Reichmann at the Nat. Inst. of Health, Bethesda, Maryland, October 1959). *Psychiatry: Journal for the Study of Interpersonal Processes, 23*/3: 231–243 [reprinted in 1968a(1), pp. 157–188].

(2)   In German: 'Der regredierte Patient und sein Analytiker'. *Psyche, 15*/5: 253–273, 1961/62 [reprinted in 1968a(3), pp. 193–228].

(3)   In French: 'La régression du patient et l'analyste'. *Psychanalyse, 7*: 313–339, 1964 (translated from the English by V. Smirnoff) [reprinted in 1968a(4), pp. 213–252, with the title 'Le patient en état de régression et son analyste'].

1960d. (1)   'Training for psychosomatic medicine', in *Fortschritte der psychosomatischen Medizin/Advances in Psychosomatic Medicine/Progrès en Médecine psy-*

chosomatique, by A. Jores & B. Stokvis (eds.), Basle/New York: Karger, pp. 167–179.

(2) American edition: A. Jores & H. Freyburger (eds.), New York: R. Brunner, pp. 167–179.

1960e. (1) 'Examination by the patient'. *Excerpta Medica*, No. 53, pp. 9–14 [reprinted in 1961a(1), pp. 47–60].

(2) In French: 'Examen du malade par lui-même' (Conference held on 11 March 1961 at the Société Française de Médecine Psychosomatique). Abstract, *Rev. Méd. Psychosom.*, *3*/2: 1–8, 1961 [also in 1961a(4), pp. 65–80].

(3) In German: 'Untersuchung durch den Patienten'. *Med. Monatsspiegel*, Heft 5, pp. 111–115, 1965 [published in 1961a(3), pp. 73–90, with the title 'Die Beteiligung des Patienten an der Untersuchung'].

1961a. (1) 'Psychotherapeutic techniques in medicine' (with Enid Balint). London: Tavistock Publications.

(2) American edition: Springfield, Ill.: Charles C Thomas, 1962.

(3) In German: *Psychotherapeutische Techniken in der Medizin*. Stuttgart: Huber, Bern/Klett-Cotta, 1962 (translated from the English by K. Hügel, 3rd edition, 1980).
In paperback edition: Munich: Kindler, 1970.

(4) In French: *Techniques psychothérapeutiques en médecine*. Paris: Payot, 1966, republished 1967, 1970, 1976 (translated from the English by J. Dupont & J. P. Valabrega).
In paperback edition: Paris: Payot, 1970.

(5) In Spanish: *Técnicas psicoterapéuticas en medicina*. Mexico City: Siglo Veintiuno Editores, 1966 (translated from the English by M. Rodriguez Cabo).

(6) In Italian: *Tecniche psicoterapiche in medicina*. Turin: Piccola Biblioteca Einaudi, 1970 (translated from the English by L. Schittar).

1961b. (1) 'The other part of medicine' (shortened version of 'The place of psychotherapy in medicine'. Paper given on 29 April 1960 at the Annual Meeting of the Deutsche Gesellschaft für Psychotherapie und

Tiefenpsychologie, Wiesbaden). *Lancet*, pp. 40–42, 7 January 1961 [also in 1961a(1), pp. 116–129].

(2) In German: 'Der Platz der Psychotherapie in der Medizin'. *Psyche, 16*/6: 355–373, 1962 [also in 1961a(3), pp. 154–171].

(3) In French: 'Place de la psychothérapie en médecine', in 1961a(4), pp. 140–155.

1961c. (1) 'Training of general practitioners and medical students in their role in mental health'. Working Paper No. 2, Committee of Experts of the Mental Health, World Health Organization, Geneva.

(2) In French: 'Comment préparer les praticiens de médecine générale et les étudiants en médecine à s'acquitter de leur rôle dans le domaine de la santé mentale'. *Praxis, 52*/41: 1231–1235, 1963.
See also 1961d.

1961d. 'The pyramid and the psychotherapeutic relationship' (shortened version of 1961c). *Lancet*, pp. 1051–1054, 11 November 1961.

1961e. (1) 'Experiences of a psychiatrist with postgraduate training of general practitioners in groups'. Abstract of *Huisarts en Wetenschap, 4*/5: 1–8.

(2) In German: 'Erfahrungen eines Psychiaters bei der Fortbildung von praktischen Aerzten im Gruppenverband', in *Medizinische Psychologie in der hausärztlichen Praxis*. Hippokrates Verlag, pp. 27–41, 1963.

1961f. (1) 'The present and the absent patient'. Report of a symposium on the emotional troubles in general practice, held at Torre Abbey, Torquay, 6 May 1961. Supplement to *J. Coll. Gen. Practitioners, 4*/4: 9–21 [published also in 1961a(1), pp. 82–103].

(2) In German: 'Der anwesende und der abwesende Patient', in 1961a(3), pp. 115–139.

(3) In French: 'Le malade présent et le malade absent', in 1961a(4), pp. 104–126.

1961g. (1) Preface to *Night Calls*, by Max B. Clyne. London: Tavistock Publications, pp. IX-X.

(2) American edition: Springfield, Ill.: Charles C Thomas, pp. IX-X, 1962.

(3)   In German: *Der Anruf bei Nacht. Eine psychologi-sche Untersuchung aus der ärztlichen Praxis.* Stutt-gart: Klett, 1964, pp. 9–11 (translated from the English by M. von Eckardt).

1962a.   (1)   'Ein Zwischenfall: Bericht über eine nichtverbale analytische Intervention'. *Jb. Psychoanal.*, *2*: 161–173, 1961/62.

(2)   In English: 'Examination of a non-verbal analytic intervention' (undated typewritten manuscript).

1962b.   (1)   'The theory of parent–infant relationship.' Contribu-tion to the Symposium of the 22nd International Congress of Psychoanalysis in Edinburgh in 1961. *Int. J. Psycho-Anal.*, *43/4–5*: 251–252 [reprinted in 1965a(1), pp. 145–147].

(2)   In German: 'Beitrag zum Symposium über die Theorie der Eltern-Kind-Beziehung', in 1965a(3), pp. 181–183.

(3)   In French: 'Contribution au Symposium sur la théorie de la relation parent-nourrisson', in 1965a(4), pp. 170–172.

1962c.   (1)   Preface to *Virgin Wives,* by Leonard J. Friedman. London: Tavistock Publications, pp. VII-X.

(2)   American edition: Springfield, Ill.: Charles C Tho-mas, pp. VII-X.

(3)   In German: *Virginität in der Ehe.* Stuttgart: Klett, 1963, pp. 7–10 (translated from the English by K. Hügel).
In paperback edition: Munich: Kindler, 1971, pp. 7–11.

1963a.   (1)   'The younger sister and prince charming'. *Int. J. Psycho-Anal.*, *44/2*: 226–227.

(2)   In Spanish: 'La hermana menor y el principe azul'. *Rev. Psiconanal.*, *22/1–2*: 10–12, 1965.

1963b.   (1)   'The malignant and the benign forms of regression'. *Bull. Ass. Psycho-Anal. Med.*, *3/2*: 20–28 [reprinted with the title: 'The benign and the malignant forms of regression' in 1968a(1), pp. 117–156, and in *New Perspectives in Psychoanalysis, Sándor Rado Lec-*

tures 1957–1963, edited by G. K. Daniels, New York: Grune & Stratton, 1965].

(2)   In French: 'Formes bénignes et malignes de la régression', in 1968a(4), pp. 161–211.

(3)   In German: 'Gutartige und bösartige Formen der Regression', in 1968a(3), pp. 143–190.

1963c.   Book review: *Adventure in Psychiatry: Social Change in a Mental Hospital,* by D. V. Martin. *Brit. Med. J.,* 23 February 1963.

1964a.   (1)   *The Doctor, His Patient and the Illness.* 2nd revised and enlarged edition (1st ed. 1957a). London: Pitman Medical, 10th edition 1984.
In paperback edition: London: Pitman Medical, 1968.

(2)   American edition: New York: International Universities Press, 1964.

(3)   In German: *Der Arzt, sein Patient und die Krankheit.* Stuttgart: Klett-Cotta, 1965 (translated from the English by K. Hügel, 5th edition 1980).
In paperback edition: Frankfurt/Main: Fischer, 1970.

(4)   In Dutch: *De dokter, de patient, de ziekte.* Anvers: Aula Boeken, 1965/Utrecht: Spectrum, 1977 (translated from the English by S. Pannekoek-Westenburg).

(5)   In French: *Le Médecin, son malade et la maladie.* Paris: Payot, 1966 (translated from the English by J. P. Valabrega).

1964b.   (1)   'Understanding the patient' (Second International Conference on Psychological Teaching for Doctors). *Praxis, 27/28:* 957–963 [also in *Medical World, 102/3:* 192–203, 1965; also in *Abbottempo, Vol. 2,* London: Interspan, 1965, pp. 9–12].

(2)   In French: 'Comment comprendre le malade', in *La formation psychologique des médecins,* edited by R. Kourilsky, J. A. Gendrot & E. Raimbault, Paris: Maloine [also in *Rev. Med. Psychosom., 7/2:* 197–211, 1965].

1964c. 'Two-way telephone system for seminars using post office trunk lines'. *Lancet*: 1293–1294, 12 December 1964.

1964d. Contribution to 'Psychiatric education' (Symposium on 14–15 March 1963 at the Psychiatric Institute, Maudsley Hospital London) edited by D. L. Davies & M. Shepherd. London: Pitman Medical.

1964e. 'Entretien avec les Drs M. Balint et P. M. Turquet. *Rev. Méd. Psychosom.*, 6/3: 327–340.

1964f. Preface to the 2nd edition of *Bausteine zur Psychoanalyse, Vol. I,* by Sándor Ferenczi. Bern/Stuttgart: Huber, pp. 7–8.

1964g. Preface to *Psychanalyse* (Oeuvres complètes) by Sándor Ferenczi, Vol. 1, Paris: Payot, 1968 (republished 1982), pp. VII–XI.

1964h. Introduction to *Advances in Psychosomatic Medicine,* edited by A. Jores & B. Stokvis. Basle/New York: Karger, 1964, pp. 1–3.

1965a. (1) *Primary Love and Psychoanalytic Technique,* 2nd revised and enlarged edition. London: Tavistock Publications (1st ed. 1952a) [reprinted London: Maresfield Library, 1985].

(2) American edition: New York: Liveright.

(3) In German: *Die Urformen der Liebe und die Technik der Psychoanalyse* Berne: Huber/Stuttgart: Klett, 1966 (translated from the English by K. Hügel & coll.).

In paperback edition: Frankfurt/M.: Fischer, 1969.

(4) In French: *Amour primaire et technique psychanalytique,* Paris: Payot, 1972 (translated from the English by J. Dupont, R. Gelly & S. Kadar).

1965b. (with Ian Hector). 'Secondary frigidity' *Medical World, 102*: 108–113.

1965c. 'Whole person medicine'. *New Soc. 131*: 16–17, 1 April 1965.

1965d. (1) 'The doctor's therapeutic function'. Address at the Second International Conference on the Training of General Practitioners, Versailles, 22 March 1964). *Lancet*, pp. 1177–1180, 5 June 1965.

(2) In French: 'La fonction thérapeutique du médecin. *Rev. méd. Psychosom.*, *8*/2: 145–154, 1966.

(3) In Hungarian: 'As orvos gyógyitó szerepének fejlö-désmenete' [The development of the therapeutic function of the doctor]. *Orvosi Hetilap*, Budapest, *106*/29: 1345–1350.

1965e. 'Zur Klinik psychosomatischer Erkrankungen'. *Helv. Med. Acta*, *32*/4–5: 374–380.

1965f. Preface to *Marriage and First Pregnancy*, by E. R. Goshen-Gottstein. London: Tavistock Publications and J. B. Lippincott, pp. IX-X.

1965g. Book review: *The Wild Analyst (G. Groddeck)*, by C. M. & S. Grossman. *New Soc. 144*: 26,1 July 1965.

1966a. (1) 'A study of doctors' (with Enid Balint, R. Gosling & P. Hildebrand). London: Tavistock Publications. Contributions of M. Balint: 'The need for selection', pp. 30–42 (Chap. 3) and 'Conclusions', pp. 106–129.

(2) American edition: Philadelphia: Lippincott.

(3) In French: *Le Médecin en formation*. Paris: Payot, 1979 (translated from the English by Th. Guichoux).

1966b. (1) 'Die technischen Experimente Sándor Ferenczis'. *Psyche, 20*/12: 904–925 (translated from the English by K. Hügel).

(2) In English: 'Sándor Ferenczi's technical experiments', in *Psychoanalytic Techniques*, edited by B. B. Wolman. New York: Basic Books, 1967, pp. 147–167.

(3) In French: 'Les expériences techniques de Sándor Ferenczi'. *Le Coq-Héron, 26*: 2–9; *27*: 2–7; *28*: 2–10, 1967 (translated by the translation team of *Le Coq-Héron*: S. Achache-Wiznitzer, J. Dupont, S. Hommel, G. Kassai, F. Samson, P. Sabourin, & B. This).

1966c. (1) 'Psychoanalysis and medical practice'. *Int. J. Psycho-Anal.*, *47*/1: 54–62.

(2) In French: 'Psychanalyse et pratique médicale'. Conference held on 9 October 1964 at the Chicago

Institute of Psychoanalysis and at the Melbourne Institute of Psychoanalysis for the 25th anniversary. *Rev. Méd. Psychom.*, 8–9/4: 243–257, 1967.

1966d. (1) 'La psychothérapie par des non-psychiatres' (with Enid Balint). *Rev. Méd. Psychosom.*, 8/1: 71–79 (translated from the English by J. Dupont & J. P. Valabrega) [already published in 1961a(4), pp. 19–27].

(2) In English: 'Psychotherapy by non-psychiatrists', in 1961a(1), pp. 3–10.

(3) In German: 'Psychotherapie durch Nicht-Psychiater', in 1961a(3), pp. 23–32.

1966e. 'The drug "doctor"', in *Medical Care. Readings in the Sociology of Medical Institutions*, edited by W. R. Scott & E. H. Volkart. New York: Wiley, pp. 281–291.

1966f. (1) Preface to *One Man's Practice*, by R. S. Greco & R. A. Pittenger. London: Tavistock Publications.

(2) American edition: Philadelphia: Lippincott.

1966g. (1) Preface to *Psychoanalyse der frühen Lebensjahre* by Alice Balint. Munich/Basle: Ernst Reinhard, pp. 7–8.

(2) In English: *The Psychoanalysis of the Nursery*. London: Routledge & Kegan Paul, 1953.

(3) American edition: *The Early Years of Life*. New York: Basic Books, 1954.

1966h. Preface to *Asthma, Attitude and Milieu*, by A. Lask. London: Tavistock Publications, Mind and Medicine Monographs, pp. IX-X.

1967a. (1) 'Philobatism and ocnophilia', in *Motivations in Play, in Games and Sports*, edited by R. Slovenko & J. A. Knight. Springfield, Ill.: Charles C Thomas, pp. 243–247 [already published in 1959a(2), pp. 26–31].

(2) In French: 'Philobatisme et ocnophilie' [already published in 1959a(4), pp. 29–36].

(3) In German: 'Philobatismus und Oknophilie' [already published in 1959a(3), pp. 23–27].

1967b. 'Médecine psychosomatique: valeur des séminaires associant l'enseignement et la recherche'. *Médecine et Hygiène, 25*: 139–140.

1967c. 'Therapeutische Regression, Urform der Liebe und die Grundstörung'. *Psyche, 21/*10–11: 713–727 [reprinted in 1968a(3), chap. 24, with the title 'Therapeutische Regression, primäre Liebe und Grundstörung'].

1967d. 'Zur Neuauflage der "Bausteine zur Psychoanalyse", von Sándor Ferenczi'. *Psyche, 21/*4: 254–255.

1967e. 'Il lavoro di gruppo,' in *La psicoterapia in Italia*, edited by P. F. Galli. Milan: La Formazione degli Psichiatri, Centro di Studi di Psicoterapia clinica.

1967f. (1) 'Mi az általános orvosi gyakorlat és mi lehetne?' *Orvosi Hetilap, 108/*21: 961–966.

    (2) In French: 'Qu'est-ce que la médecine générale et que pourrait-elle être? *Médecine et Hygiène, 26*: 124–127, 1968.

1967g. Interview: 'Psychiatrist-physician relations discussed by Dr. Michael Balint', in *Roche Report: Frontiers of Clinical Psychiatry, Vol. 4*, No. 7, pp. 1–8.

1967h. 'La formazione psicologica del medico'. Panel at the First National Congress of the Italian Society of Psychosomatic Medicine, Rome, 11–14 September 1967.

1967i. Book review: *Sick Humans: Doctors and Patients*, by M. Hodson, *New Soc. 250*: 57, 14 July 1967.

1967j. Book review: *Personality and Arousal*, by C. S. Claridge. *New Soc., 266*: 642, 2 November 1967.

1967k. Book review: *Psychoanalytic Pioneers*, edited by F. Alexander, S. Eisenstein & M. Grotjahn. *Psychoanal. Forum, 2/*4: 373–375.

1968a (1) *The Basic Fault: Therapeutic Aspects of Regression.* London: Tavistock Publications.

    (2) For the United States: distribution by Barnes & Noble Inc.

    (3) In German: *Therapeutische Aspekte der Regression. Die Theorie der Grundstó4rung.* Reinbek/Hamburg: Rowohlt, 1973 (translated from the English by K. Hügel).
    Paperback: Stuttgart: Klett, 1970.

(4)　In French: *Le défaut fondamental. Aspects thérapeutiques de la régression.* Paris: Payot, 1971, 1977, 1979 (translated from the English by J. Dupont & M. Viliker).
Paperback: Paris: Payot, 1979.

1968b.　(1)　'The structure of the training-cum-research seminars and its implications for medicine', in *Proceedings of the Seventh APA Colloquium for Postgraduate Teaching of Psychiatry, New Orleans,* pp. 5–18 [reprinted in *J. Roy. Coll. Gen. Practit., 17/81:* 201–211, 1969] (paper also given at the Seventh International Congress of Psychotherapy in Wiesbaden, 1967).

(2)　In German: 'Die Struktur der Training-cum-Research Gruppen und deren Auswirkungen auf die Medizin'. *Jb. Psychoanal., 5:* 125–146.

(3)　In French: 'Les séminaires de formation et recherche: leurs structures et leurs implications en médecine'. *Rev. Méd. Psychosom., 10/4:* 367–391 (translated from the English by J. Morche).

1968c.　'Erfahrungen mit Ausbildungs- und Forschungs-Seminaren'. Contribution to a Symposium on the training of psychiatrists of the Gruppo Milanese per lo Sviluppo della Psicoterapia, November 1966. *Psyche, 22/9–11:* 679–688 (translated by J. Bally).

1968d.　'Medicine and psychosomatic medicine. New possibilities in training and practice'. *Compr. Psychiat., 9/4:* 267–274.

1968e.　Preface to *Sexual Discord in Marriage,* by M. Courtenay. London: Tavistock Publications and J. B. Lippincott, pp. IX–XII.

1968f.　'Letter to the Editor'. *Int. J. Psycho-Anal., 49/1:* 99.

1968g.　Book Review: *Adventure in Psychiatry: Social Change in a Mental Hospital* (2nd edition) by D. V. Martin. *Brit. Med. J.,* 13 July 1968.

1969a.　(1)　'Trauma and object relationship'. *Int. J. Psycho-*

Anal., *50*/4: 429–435. Also in *Brit. Psychoanal. Soc. Bull.*, *34*: 1–16.

(2)   In German: 'Trauma und Objektbeziehung'. *Psyche, 24*/5: 346–358, 1970 (translated from the English by K. Hügel).

1969b. (1)   'Training medical students in patient-centered medicine' (with D. H. Ball & M. L. Hare). *Compr. Psychiat.*, *10*/4: 249–258 [also in 'Synapse', *J. Edinburgh Med. School.*, *20*/2: 17–23, 1970, with the title: 'Teaching patient-centred medicine'].

(2)   In German: 'Unterrichtung von Medizinstudenten in patientenzentrierter Medizin'. *Psyche, 23*/7: 532–546 (translated from the English by L. Rosenkötter).

(3)   In French: 'Formation des étudiants en médecine à la médecine centrée sur le malade'. *Rev. Méd. Psychosom.*, *12*/2: 131–143, 1970.

1969c.   'Pädiatrie und Psychotherapie in der ärztlichen Praxis. Erfahrungen mit Aerzteseminaren', in *Handbuch der Kinderpsychotherapie*, edited by G. Biermann. Munich/ Basle: Ernst Reinhardt, pp. 1030–1036 (translation of a contribution in English to a unpublished discussion at the British Paediatry Association in 1961).

1969d.   'Thoughts on the problem of the membership of the society'. *President's News Bull.*, *13*: 3–15.

1969e.   'The problem of membership: The next steps'. *President's News Bull.*, *14*: 2–3.

1969f.   'The discussions in the scientific meetings of our society'. *President's News Bull.*, 16: 2–3.

1969g.   Editorial: 'L'approche du malade' (with B. Luban-Plozza). *Médecine et Hygiène, 27*: 121–122.

1969h.   Collaboration in *Jahrbuch der Psychoanalyse. Beiträge zur Theorie und Praxis*. Band 6, edited by K. Dräger, E. Meistermann, A. Mitscherlich, P. Parin, H. E. Richter, G. Scheunert & W. Solms-Rödelheim. Berne/Stuttgart/ Vienna: Huber.

1969i.   'Introduction to "Journal de S. Ferenczi"', in *Journal clinique (janvier–octobre 1932)*, by S. Ferenczi. Paris:

Payot, 1985, pp. 13–15 (translated from the German by the translation team of *Le Coq-Héron*—see 1966b).

1969j. 'Notes pour une préface,' in *Journal clinique (janvier–octobre 1932)*, by S. Ferenczi. Paris: Payot, 1985, pp. 16–18 (translated from the German by the translation team of *Le Coq-Héron*,—see 1966b).

1969k. Book review: *Beyond the Therapeutic Community. Social Learning and Social Psychiatry*, by M. Jones. *Brit. Med. J., 1*: 304–305, 1 February 1969.

1969l. Book review: *Sex and Society in Sweden*, by B. Linner. *Brit. Med. J., 2*: 564, 5 April 1969.

1969m. Book review: *The Hostage Seekers: A Study of Childless and Adopting Couples*, by M. Humphrey. *Brit. Med. J., 4*: 218, 4 October 1969.

1970a. (1) 'Treatment or diagnosis: A study of repeat prescriptions in general practice' (with J. Hunt, D. Joyce, M. Marinker & J. Woodcock). *Mind and Medicine Monographs*, London: Tavistock Publications.

(2) American edition: Philadelphia/Toronto: Lippincott.

(3) In German: 'Das Wiederholungsrezept: Behandlung oder Diagnose?'. Stuttgart: Klett, 1975 (translated from the English by K. Hügel).

1970b. (1) 'Repeat prescription patients: Are they an identifiable group?' *Psychiat. in Med., 1*/1: 3–14 [also in 1970a(1), Chap. 2, pp. 18–47].

(2) In German: 'Bilden die langfristig mit den gleichen Rezepten versorgten Patienten eine identifizierbare Gruppe?'. *Psyche, 27*/2: 101–117, 1973 (translated from the English by K. Hügel).

1970c. 'La genèse de mes idées'. *Gaz. Méd. France, 77*/3: 457–466.

1970d. (1) 'Research in psychotherapy and the importance of the findings for psychoanalysis'. Paper given at the International Congress of the French Society of Psychosomatic Medicine, Paris, September 1970. *Rev. Méd. Psychosom., 10*/3: 225–240 [reprinted in Proceedings of the Fourth Int. Congr. Psychosom., in *Med., Psychother. Psychosom., 21*/1: 9–27, 1972/73, reprinted in *Psychotherapeutic Action of the Physi-*

cian/Action psychothérapeutique du médecin, edited by L. Chertok & M. Sapir. Basle: Karger, 1973].

(2)   In French: 'Recherches sur la psychothérapie et importance des résultats pour la psychanalyse' (translated from the English by J. Morche). *Rev. Méd. Psychosom., 13*/1: 55–72, 1971.

(3)   In German: 'Psychotherapeutische Forschung und ihre Bedeutung für die Psychoanalyse'. *Psyche, 26*/1: 1–19, 1972 (translated from the English by J. Bally).

1970e.   Editing of *Schriften zur Psychoanalyse, Vol. 1,* by S. Ferenczi. Frankfurt/Main: S. Fischer.

Preface: *Sándor Ferenczi,* 'Einleitung des Herausgebers', pp. IX–XXII.

1970f.   Preface to *Psychanalyse (Oeuvres complètes), Vol. 2,* by S. Ferenczi. Paris: Payot, 1970 and 1978, pp. 7–10 (translated from the English by J. Dupont & M. Viliker, with the collaboration of Ph. Garnier).

1971a.   'Les interruptions de grossesse vécues par le médecin de famille en Grande-Bretagne' (with A. M. Sandler). *Gaz. Méd. France, 78*/4: 509–516.

1971b.   'Ichstärke, Ichpädagogik und "Lernen"' (see also 1939b), in *Psychoanalyse und Erziehungspraxis,* edited by J. Cremerius. Frankfurt/Main: Fischer, pp. 92–102 [reprinted in *Psychologie des Ich. Psychoanalytische Ich-Psychologie und ihre Anwendungen (Wege der Forschung, Bd. 259),* edited by P. Kutter & H. Roskamp. Darmstadt: Wissenschaftliche Buchgesellschaft, 1974, XIII, pp. 91–104].

1971c.   'The family doctor and patient's secrets'. *Psychiat. in Med., 2*: 98–107.

1971d.   'The family and its doctor'. Abstract, *Scient. Bull., 53*: 1–15 [also in *Psychiat. in Med., 2*: 98–107].

1972a.   (1)   *Focal Psychotherapy—An Example of Applied Psychoanalysis* (with P. H. Ornstein & Enid Balint). London: Tavistock Publications, and Philadelphia/Toronto: Lippincott.

(2) In German: *Fokaltherapie. Ein Beispiel angewandter Psychoanalyse.* Frankfurt/Main: Suhrkamp, 1973 (translated from the English by K. Hügel). Paperback, Suhrkamp, in press.

(3) In Italian: *La psicoterapia focale. Un esempio di psicoterapia applicata.* Rome: Casa Editrice Astrolabio Ubeldini Editore, 1974 (translated from the English by M. Cuzzolaro).

(4) In French: *La psychothérapie focale. Un exemple de psychanalyse appliquée.* Paris: Payot, 1975 (translated from the English by J. Dupont & R. Gelly).

1972b. Contribution to the discussion on 'Supervision by Tape: A New Method of Case Supervision', by J. A. Lindon, in *Psychoanal. Forum, Vol. 4,* edited by J. A. Lindon. New York: International Universities Press, pp. 419–422.

1972c. Recorded interview in *Patient-centred Medicine,* edited by Ph. Hopkins. London: Regional Doctor Publications, p. 316.

1972d. Editing of *Schriften zur Psychoanalyse, Vol. II,* by S. Ferenczi. Frankfurt/Main: S. Fischer (Introduction by J. Dupont).

1973a. (1) 'Research in psychotherapy' (modified version of 1970d), in *Six Minutes for the Patient: Interactions in General Practice Consultation,* edited by Enid Balint & J. S. Norell. London/New York: Tavistock Publications, pp. 1–18.

(2) In German: 'Forschung in der Psychotherapie', in *Fünf Minuten pro Patient. Eine Studie über die Interaktionen in der ärztlichen Allgemeinpraxis.* Frankfurt/Main: Suhrkamp, 1975, pp. 35–57 (translated from the English by K. Hügel).

(3) In French: 'La recherche en psychothérapie', in *Six minutes par patient. Interactions en consultation de médecine générale.* Paris: Payot, 1976, pp. 27–48 (translated from the English by R. Barisse).

1974a. (1) Preface to *Psychosomatic Disorders in General Practice* by B. Luban-Plozza & W. Pó4ldinger. Basle: Editions Roche, pp. 11–13.

(2)   In French: Preface to *Le malade psychosomatique et
le médecin praticien*. Basle: Ed. Roche, pp. 7–9.

1986a. 'Considérations au sujet du développement mental pré-
coce, du traumatisme et d'une nouvelle science appelée
"pédagogie expérimentale"' (fragments published by A.
Haynal). *Le Bloc-Notes de la Psychanalyse*, No. 6. Geneva:
Georg (translated from the English by M. G. Sorrentino).

*Papers, unpublished or without publication references (Balint
Archives, Geneva)*

Book review: *The Teaching and Learning of Psychotherapy*, by R.
Ekstein and R. S. Wallerstein (New York: Basic Books, 1958).

Interview of 6–7 August 1965, by Bluma Swerdloff (New York:
Columbia University, Oral History Research Office).

Book review: *Psychotherapy: Myth and Method*, by I. Ehrenwald
(Orlando, Florida: Grune & Stratton, 1966).

'Réunion du 13–14 Août 1968' (case conference by Dr. Balint with
various doctors).

Book review: *The Psychoanalytic Revolution—Sigmund Freud's
Life and Achievement*, by Marthe Robert (undated).

Some general remarks on over-eating and obesity (undated).

Discrete and continuous—man's eternal need for paradoxes and
contradictions (undated).

The place of psychology in education (undated).

Notes on phallo- and gynecocentrism (undated).

The spelling of Hungarian names

We have not always maintained the correct Hungarian spelling of Hungarian names, since Hungarians outside their country have frequently dropped the accents, or some of the accents, from their names, even though they had used them earlier in their lives and continued to use them in a Hungarian context (Kovacs, Koranyi instead of Kovács, Korányi). Some authors kept the accents on their names in the works of their youth (e.g. Bálint, Szász), but dropped them in their later work (Balint, Szasz). Some accents are retained more easily than others—e.g. Béla Bartok (the 'e' with accent and the 'o' without, evidently for typographical reasons, as more languages use an 'e' with and accent than an 'a' or an 'o'). We have endeavoured to reproduce the names in the form in which they are most widely known.

INDEX

Abraham, K., 6, 9, 11, 57, 59, 95, 99, 106

Adler, A. 42, 138

Ady, E., 48

Alexander, F., xii, 13, 38, 46, 49, 58, 113, 143

Almássy, E., 47

alpha elements (Bion), 89

analysis
  aims of, 72
  focus of, 129

analyst, part of in psychoanalysis, 67–69

analysts
  controversies between, xi, xii, 67–69, 134–43
    in the 1920s and 1930s, 65–66

Aristotle, 100

Assoun, P., xv

Aster Revolution, 104

Austrian National Library, xvii, 59

Bachelard, G., 1

Bak, R., xii, 38, 47, 108

Balazs, B., 37, 48

Balint, A. (née Székely-Kovacs), 33, 38, 69, 72, 77, 80, 98, 104, 105, 106, 107, 110, 111, 128

Balint, E. F. (Eichholz, née Albu), xvii, 112–15, 117, 118–19,

Balint, Emmi, 104

Balint, J., 111

Balint, M., xi, xii, xvi, xvii, 20, 23, 25–26, 29, 39, 41, 43, 46, 50, 55, 58, 68, 71–125, 128, 132, 134, 139, 140, 142, 143
  Archives, xii, xvii, xviii, 82

195

bibliography of the works of,
163–91
family history of, 103–4
Groups, 93
life of, 103–21
in England, 111–21
personality of, 121–23
Bartók, B., 37, 38, 48, 58
Benedek, T., xii, 46
Berényi, R., 110
Berlin
Institute, 45, 95
School, 57
Bernheim, xv
Beta elements (Bion), 89
Bibring, G., 65
Bion, W. R., 65, 89, 113, 114,
124
Blanton, S., 2, 10, 11
Boss, M., 12
Braham, R. L., 59
Breuer, 31, 32
British Middle Group, xvi, 123
British Psychoanalytical Soci-
ety, 75, 112, 116, 118, 139
British Psychological Society,
Medical Section, 116
Brücke, xv, 3
Budapest
Congress (1918), 22, 44, 45,
90
emigration of intellectuals
from, 38–39, 46–47, 49
importance of, xiii
influence of in psychoanaly-
sis, xii
intellectual circles in, 47–48
Psychoanalytic Institute, 108
School, xi, xii, xiv, xvii, 93

character analysis, psychoana-
lysis as (Reich), 62–63
Charcot, J. M., xv
Charité Hospital, Berlin, 106,
124
Charles III of Hungary
(Charles VI of Austria),
35
Chertok, L., xv
Chislehurst Child Guidance
Clinic, 111
clinging instinct, concept of
(Hermann), 46
Clyne, M., 113
Comte, A., xv
Congresses of the International
Psychoanalytical Asso-
ciation, 161–62
content, vs. process, xiii
counter-transference, 2
(Balint), 76–77
(Ferenczi), 20
(Freud), 2–3, 11–16
County Borough of Preston
Child Guidance Clinic,
111
Courtenay, M., 113
Cremerius, J., 123

Darwin, C., xv
De Saussure, R., xv
Dénes, Zs., 52
defence (A. Freud), 63
dependability of analyst
(Ferenczi), 27
Deutsch, H., 57, 106
Dicks, H. V., 114
Doolittle, H., 7, 8
Dormandi, O., 103, 112

dreams
  communicative value of
    (Ferenczi), 19–20
  Freud's study of, 3
Dukész, G., 108
Dupont, J., xvii, 33, 34, 44, 45,
    53, 58

Eichenburg, H. B., 12
Einstein, A., 1, 37
Eissler, K., 134
Eitigon, M., 49, 56, 106
Ellenberger, H., xv
empathy
  importance of (Ferenczi), 24
  vs. interpretation, xiii
English Middle Group, 134
experience
  direct, vs. insight, xiii
  importance of (Ferenczi), 20–
    21
  role of over theoretical ab-
    stractions (Balint), 99

Fairbairn, 99
Family Discussion Bureau, 115
Family Welfare Association,
    114
Farkasházy, M., 108
Fechner, xv
Federn, P. 21
Feldman, S., xii, 38, 46
Felszeghy, R. (Mrs.), 108
Fenichel, O., 21, 61, 66–67, 68,
    98, 111
Fenyö, M., 48
Ferdinand the First, 35
Ferenczi, S., xii, xiii, xvi, xvii,
    4, 13–14, 16–18, 19–59,

62, 63, 66, 68, 72, 75, 76,
    79, 83, 84, 89, 91, 92, 94–
    97, 101, 102, 104, 106,
    108, 109, 112, 113, 115,
    123, 124, 128–30, 132–
    34, 136–43
  –Abraham controversy, 57
  and Balint, differences
    between, 132
  family history of, 38–39
  Freud
    friendship with, 39–45
    controversy, see Freud–
      Ferenczi controversy
  –Jones controversy, 55–56
  last illness of, 53–55
  personal life of, 39–58
Feuerbach, 3
First Psychoanalytic Congress,
    Vienna, 39
Fischer, G., 39
Fliess, W., 3, 41, 136
Forel, A., 31
Forest, I. de, 52, 143
Franz Joseph of Austria, 38, 48,
    58
Franz Liszt Academy of Music,
    58
Freud, A., 12, 26, 63, 113
Freud, S. xi, xii, xiii, xv, xvi,
    xvii, 1–18, 19, 21, 22, 24,
    25, 29, 31–33, 35–58, 61,
    62, 65, 67, 69, 72, 76, 77,
    85, 86, 91, 92, 94–97, 101,
    111, 118, 127, 128, 132–
    42
  contradiction between posi-
    tion and practice, 2
  –Ferenczi

controversy, xiii, 16–18,
    30–33, 50–58, 94–95,
    127–28, 134–35
correspondence, xii, 41–42,
    49, 115
Correspondence, Committee
    for the Publication
    of, xvii
friendship, 39–45
Freund (-Tószeghy), Anton von,
    42, 46
Friedrich, L., 108
Frigyes, A., 48
Fromm, E., 52, 96

Galileo Circle, 48
Gedo, J., xii, 11, 46
George, S., 48
Gill, C. H., 113
Gill, M., 4
Girard, C., 58
Glover, E., 55, 62, 65–66, 75, 81
Gömbös, 36, 109
Gömbös, 36
Goethe, J. W. von, xv
Goldberg, A., 11
Gosling, R., 114, 117
Grinker, R. R., 12
Groddeck, G., 1, 3, 14, 17, 26,
    44, 49, 50, 51, 52
Grosskurth, Ph., 59
Grotjahn, M., 59, 82
Grubrich-Simitis, I., xvii, 24,
    25, 29, 39–41
Grunberger, B., 39, 52
Gyömröi, E. (Ludowyk-), 38, 46,
    48, 108

Hajdu, L., 47, 108
Harnik, J., 38, 46, 49, 106

healing (Ferenczi), 21
Hegel, 140
Heimann, P., 128, 134
Heine, H., 39
Helmholtz, 3
Hermann, A., 46
Hermann, I., 38, 46, 48, 54, 58,
    105–6, 108
Hevesi, S., 47
Hildebrand, 117
His, W., 124
Hollós, I., 42, 45, 59, 111
Horthy, M., 36, 37, 43, 48
Hungarian Medical Academy,
    120
Hungarian Medical Society, 49
Hungarian National Theatre,
    47
Hungarian Psychoanalytical
    Group, 130–31
Hungarian Psychoanalytical
    Society, 42, 46, 108, 124
Hungarian Reawakening
    movement, 106
Hungary
    exodus of intellectuals from,
        38–39, 46–47, 49
    history of (1529–1948), 35–38
hypnosis, 2
    (Ferenczi), 20, 39
    (Freud), 2–3, 5

ideas, history of, xvi
Ignotus, H., 42, 47, 48
Ignotus, P., 113
Independent Group, 143
Independents, vs. Freudians
    and Kleinians, xvi
infant
    interaction with mother, xiii

–parent relationship (Fe-
 renczi), 79–80
infantile mental development
 (Balint), 79–80
insight, vs. direct experience,
 xiii
Institute of Marital Studies,
 115
International Psychoanalytical
 Association, 27, 42, 44–
 45, 51, 52, 134, 137,
 Congresses of, 161–62
International Psychological Association, 27–28
interpretation
 vs. empathy, xiii
 role of (Glover), 66–67
introjection (Sterba), 65

Jacoby, R., 98, 111
Joffe, W. G., 113, 123
Jones, E., 30, 34, 41, 50, 54, 55,
 57–59, 89, 95, 96, 104,
 111, 113, 136–38,
Joseph II of Austria, 103
Jozsef, A., 36, 47
Jung, C. G., 42, 54, 135, 136,
 138

Károlyi, 'Red' Count, 43
Kafka, F., 37
Kaiser, H., 64
Kant, I., xv, 3, 38
Kanzer, M., 11
Karadi, E., 48
Kardiner, A., 4, 11, 12
Karinthy, F., 47
Karolyi, 36
Kaufmann, W., xv
Kentner, L., 113, 125

Khan, M. M. R., 9–10, 79, 102,
 124
Kierkegaard, S. A., 48
Klein, M., xiii, 3, 49, 57, 59, 65,
 78, 81, 82, 84, 95, 106,
 113, 128, 133, 138
Kleinian School, 79, 86, 143
Kodaly, Z., 48
Koestler, A., 37
Kohut, H., xiii, 99, 124
Koranyi, 108
Kosztolányi, D., 47, 48
Kovacs, F., 108, 109
Kovacs, V., 68, 72, 108–9, 136
Kris, E., 10–11, 88
Kun, B., 36, 43, 105
Kunfi, Zs., 43

Lacan, xiii, 99
Lagache, D., 82, 139
Lampl-de Groot, J., 8
language, and translation
 problems (Balint), 86
Lévy, K., 46
Lévy, L., 42, 46
Levine, M., 113
Lichtenberg, 3
Lipton, S., 4, 7
Little, M., 102, 124
Lobner, H., 63
Loch, 117
London Congress (1953), 123
Lorand, S., xii, 21, 38, 47, 54,
 143
Lorenz, P., 7
Lorin, C., 27, 92
Luban-Plozza, B., 113
Lukacs, D., 48
Lukacs, G., 37, 38, 47

Mahler, M., xiii, 104, 124, 143
Main, T., 113
Manchester Northern Royal
    Hospital, 111
Manchester, University of,
    111–12
Mannheim, K., 48
Maria Theresa of Austria, 35
Marx, K., 100
Masson, J. M., 30–31, 33, 41,
    51, 113
maturation, zones of (Balint),
    85–89
McDougall, J., 64
Meltzer, D., 124
Menuhin, Y., 113
metapsychological tradition
    (Balint), 97–98
metapsychology
    of analyst's mental processes
        (Ferenczi), 23–24
    vs. technique, xiii
method, psychoanalysis as, xv
Mill, J. S., xv
Miller, A., 34
Mitscherlich, 117
Molnar, M., 124
Money-Kyrle, R. E., 7–8
Moravcsik, 45
mother, interaction of with in-
    fant, xiii
mourning (Balint), 80–83
Munich Congress (1913), 68,
    136

Nacht, S., 124
narcissism, concept of (Balint),
    99
Natterson, J. M., 13
Nemes, L., 47

Nietzsche, F., xv, 3
Norrell, J. S., 117
North East Lancashire Child
    Guidance Clinic, 111
Nunberg, 69
Nuremberg Congress (1910), 42

Oakeshott, E., 112
object-relationship, and intra-
    analytic relationship
    (Balint), 80–81
ocnophilia
    (Balint), 84, 128
    (Hermann), 46
Ornstein, A., 113
Ornstein, P., 113, 117
Osvát, E., 48

Palos, E., 31, 43
Palos, G., 43, 44
Paterson, M., xvii
Pfeiffer, S., 108
Pfister, 6
philobatism
    (Balint), 84, 128
    (Hermann), 46
physicians, psychoanalytic
    training of (Balint), 92–
    94
Plato, 100
Polanyi, M., 48
Pontalis, J.-B., 100
primary love (Balint), 80
psychoanalysis
    and character analysis (Ba-
        lint), 71–72
    controversies in, xi, xiii, 65–
        69, 134–43
    developments in, xvi
    guidelines for (Freud), 1–17

as method, xv
recent trends in, 133–34
training in (Balint), 89–92
Psychoanalytic Out-patient
    Clinic, Budapest, 108
Psychoanalytic Policlinic, 50
Psychoanalytic Society and In-
    stitute, Columbia Uni-
    versity, 46
Psychoanalytical Society, 124
psychology
    Freud's avoidance of, 7
    two-person, xiii

Racker, H., 134
Rado, S., xii, 42, 46, 49, 58, 105,
    143
Rajka, T., 39
Rank, O., 6, 32, 42, 49, 50, 72,
    84, 95
Rapaport, D., xii, 38, 47
Rat Man, 6, 7, 10, 22
Révész, G., 43, 58
Révész, L., 108
regression
    in analysis, study of (Balint),
        83
    (Balint), 87–88, 128
    place of in analysis, Ferenczi
        on, 6
regression
    role of (Balint), 82
    zones of (Balint), 85–89
regressive states, verbal ex-
        pression in (Balint), 86–
        87
Reich, W., 42, 57, 62–64, 72, 98
Reik, T., 13, 65, 67
Research cum Training semi-
        nars, 115

resistance, 64
    expressed in transference
        (Strachey), 64
        (Ferenczi), 21–22
        (Freud), 1
    role of, 61–63
Reverzy-Piguet, C., 20–21
Rickman, J., 12, 38, 78, 111,
    113
Rippl-Ronay, 111
Róheim, G., xii, 38, 43, 47, 98,
    108, 111, 143
Roazen, P., 55
Rona, P., 124
Rosenthal, A., xvii
Ruitenbeek, H. M., 8

Sabourin, P., 34, 59, 102
Sachs, H., 105, 106
Sandler, J., 134
Sapir, M., 113
Saussure, R. de, 10
Schoenberg,, 37
scientific theory
    (Balint), 97–98
    vs. patient's subjectivity, xiii
Searles, H., 102, 124
Severn, E., 143
Simmel, 48
Society for Social Sciences, 48
Spielrein, S., 31
Spira, M., 3
Spitz, R. A., xiii, 38, 48, 124,
    143
splitting (Ferenczi), 29
Stein, F., 39
Stekel, 51, 138
Sterba, R. F., 57, 62, 63, 65, 66,
    95
Strachey, A., 8–9

Strachey, J., 12, 55, 64
subjectivity, patient's, vs.
    'scientific' theory, xiii
Sullivan, H. S., xvii
Sunday Circle, The, 48
surprise, role of (Reik), 65
Sutherland, J. D., 112, 113
Szasz, T., xii, 46
Székely, L., 37, 47
Szegö, J., 58
Szilard, L., 38
Szondi test, 123

Tarachow, S., 78
Tavistock
  Clinic, 112, 114–15
  Institute of Human Rela-
      tions, 114–15
technique
  analytic (Ferenczi), 22–27
  (Ferenczi), 29–34, 63
  (Reich), 63
  psychoanalytic
      (Balint), 78–79
      (Freud), 2–4
  vs. metapsychology, xiii
  questions about, 2
theory, relationship of to tech-
    nique (Ferenczi), 29
therapeutic problems, lack of
    interest in (Freud), 3–4
Thompson, C., 30, 143
Tolnay, C. de, 48
Tompa, M., 39
Torok, M. 30
transference, 1, 2, 5–7
  (Balint), 72–75

central issue in psychoanaly-
    sis (Freud), 128
–countertransference, vs.
    real relationship, xiii
  (Ferenczi), 19–21
  and resistance, 61–63
two-person psychology, xiii

unconscious, psychoanalysts'
    exploration of, 61–63
University College Hospital,
    London, 115, 124
University Hospital, Budapest,
    106

Varga, J., 48
Varo, G., 110
Veszy-Wagner, L., 46
Vezér, E., 48

Waelder, 79
Warburg, O., 106
Washington School, xvii
Weiss, E., 139–40
Wiener, L., 110
Wiesbaden Congress (1932), 71
Will, H., 3
Winnicott, D. W., xiii, 102, 124,
    128, 134
Wittgenstein, 37
Wolf Man, 11, 127

Zetzel, E. R., 11
Zondeck, 124
Zurich
  Congress, 77
  School, 57

In his foreword to *Controversies in Psychoanalytic Method*, Daniel Stern writes:

"André Haynal gives us a perspective on the history of psychoanalysis, and much more, in this multi-faceted and remarkable book. Several stories and lines of enquiry are woven together. There is the story of the Budapest school of psychoanalysis and its impact. Within and around that story, there are accounts of the lives and works of Ferenczi and Balint who provided the core of the Budapest school".

"And this brings us to the great controversy that began between Freud and Ferenczi, and was continued in the work of Balint.

Haynal describes this controversy in terms of the initial form it took; a disagreement about experimenting with technique, and Ferenczi's placing the analytic situation more squarely at the centre of the enquiry... But most valuable of all, he then elaborates upon the full implications of the controversy, and we discover this split to be at the heart of the major questions still at issue in psychoanalysis: Emphasis on technique vs. on metapsychology; direct experience vs. insight; process vs. content; the patient's subjectivity vs. the 'scientific' theory; empathy vs. interpretation; a psychology of one person (the patient) vs. a psychology of two people, the patient-therapist dyad; transference-countertransference and the 'real' relationship".

"André Haynal examines the historical roots of these problems from a fresh perspective, made possible by recent publications and by some unpublished material — the vast correspondence between Freud and Ferenczi, and valuable documents given to the Balint Archives in Geneva by Enid Balint Edmonds. The enquiry ranges from Budapest and Ferenczi to London and Michael Balint".

"In this light, the seminal importance of the Budapest school takes on larger dimensions, and we are forced to re-evaluate, in part, our intellectual ancestry".

NEW YORK UNIVERSITY PRESS
Washington Square
New York, NY 10003

Cover designed by Malcolm Smith   ISBN 0-8147-3464